it all started with a line

Disembodiment

jovis

José Salinas | KNOBSDesign
Disembodiment

a:p   architektur:positionen

Isolde Nagel [Ed.]

jovis

The series ◼:◗ architektur:positionen is edited by
Christiane Fath and Jochen Visscher

Contents

The "Double Murder" Effect in José Salinas's Work

Anh-Linh Ngo

This book offers a comprehensive overview of José Salinas's work, which includes a wide range of different approaches to architecture: architectural concepts, built projects, installations, exhibitions as well as theoretical texts. Despite their diversity, these approaches have a common issue—a deep interest in the relation between architecture and the media linked to its production. First and foremost, it is a media theoretical reflection concerning the impact of the computer on the architectural practice. As a specialist in computing, Salinas rejects using the computer merely as a tool of representation. He deeply engages in understanding the implications of the digital tools on our way of conceptualizing space and architecture.

It is commonplace that the tools we use have an impact on the artifacts we produce. But if we identify architectural tools as a media issue, then we obviously have to analyze the nature of the relationship and the effects media and architecture have on each other. In order to understand this problem, we have to go further back in history and look at the first media complex introduced in modern times: the printing press and architecture.

According to architectural theoreticians like Mario Carpo, Renaissance Architecture was influenced to a great extent by the invention of the printing press.[1] The matrix or *cliché*, i.e., the printer's stereotype of the alphabet or block of images introduced a new organizational order, which implies that a book of the same print run is a redundant matter: a book is a book is a book. The printed book with its layout, typography, and images can be reproduced in a way that the replica is indiscernible to the "original." Interestingly, with the emergence of the printing press, architectural theory found an adequate medium to disseminate architectural orders, thereby establishing a normative thinking unknown to architecture at that time. Thus, the idea of architecture as something that can be organized in standards and orders, which can

1 Cf. Mario Carpo, *Paper Palaces. The Rise of the Renaissance Architectural Treatise*, edited by Vaughan Hart and Peter Hicks. New Haven, London 1998

be repeated identically in any place at any time, is a concept inherent to the technique of printing. From this perspective, Modernism's obsession with standards, repetition, and iteration as *the* paradigm of architecture has its starting point here. But the printed book does not only standardize the language of architectural orders by disseminating replicable images. To a certain degree, it also changes the human way of thinking: from thinking in similar patterns to thinking in identical iterations. While architectural production relied for a long time on what we would today call algorithmic and generative design patterns—as the seminal research of Saverio Muratori and Gianfranco Caniggia on building typology and building practice in Venice has revealed[2]—the architecture in the age of printing tends to follow an exact order or standard.

It is noteworthy that it was not an architectural theoretician but a novelist who was the first to see a particular relationship between the printed book and architecture. In his famous novel, *Notre-Dame de Paris*, also known as *The Hunchback of Notre Dame*, Victor Hugo reflected on this very problem. Curiously, in this novel it is architecture—i.e., the church of Notre-Dame—that plays the major role and not the hunchback, as the more popular title suggests. Hugo is reflecting on the emergence of the printing press, which according to him has not only changed the notion of architecture radically, but even killed it.

The chapter begins with a dramatic scene in which the archdeacon of Notre Dame acknowledges that the printed book will not only endanger his power as a priest, but also the role of architecture as a medium:

"And opening the window of his cell, he pointed out with his finger the immense church of Notre-Dame. …

The archdeacon gazed at the gigantic edifice for some time in silence, then extending his right hand, with a sigh, towards the printed book which lay open on the table, and his left towards Notre-Dame, and turning a sad glance from the book to the church,
–'Alas,' he said, 'this will kill that.'…

To our mind, this thought had two faces. It meant, 'The press will kill the church.'

But underlying this thought, the first and most simple one, no doubt, there was in our opinion another, newer one. …

It was a presentiment that human thought, in changing its form, was about to change its mode of expression; that the book of stone, so solid and so durable, was about to make way for the book of paper, more solid and still more durable. In this connection, the archdeacon's vague formula had a second sense.

It meant, 'Printing will kill architecture.'"[3]
The quotation from Victor Hugo's *Notre-Dame de Paris* is part of a chapter that contains one of the first media theoretical reflections of our time. Basically, Victor Hugo is saying that if the media in which we express ourselves changes, this change will have a consequence for the form (*matter*) and the way (*manner*) of our articulation. If the emergence of the book as a non-permanent but infinitely replicable medium has such a fundamental change on architecture as one of the most durable media, what impact does digital media have today in relation to print media and to architecture? Put another way: what does the sentence, "This will kill that,"

2 Cf. Peter Trummer, "Vom Typus zur Population," in: *ARCH+* 189 Entwurfsmuster (Design Patterns). October 2008, pp. 46–51
3 Cf. Victor Hugo, *Notre Dame de Paris (also: The Hunchback of Notre Dame)*, translated by Isabel F. Hapgood (1896), Book 5 Excerpts from Chapter I and II, http://www.gutenberg.org/etext/2610

mean for us today? That the computer will kill the book, which in turn has killed architecture? That this "double murder" might have the effect of a double negation and in the end architecture will rise from the dead?

When the digital revolution began to reshape architecture, there was a need to re-theorize architectural thinking. In this respect, Deleuze was the man of the hour, and Leibniz's ontology as well as the rediscovering of non-Euclidean geometries of the nineteenth century were crucial references during the 1990s, which helped to understand and to operate the new tools provided by computer-aided design (CAD) and computer-aided manufacturing (CAM). But apart from and despite such takes on a new foundation for architecture, these historical references cannot conceal that the whole discipline is still lacking a methodological framework or a theoretical underpinning with regard to the ground-shaking character of the digital revolution. The question of what to do with these new tools remained unanswered for a long time. The result was an architectural practice that was obsessed with creating ever glossier images—its only driving force being the technological advancement according to Moore's law. In this situation, architecture behaved much like a kid that grows up too fast, just to find itself in a developed body that is oddly unconnected to its immature mental state.

In this context, José Salinas's experiments become a tool for grasping the newness of the digital media, not merely as a representational matter but as a conceptual practice—conceptual not in the sense of being purely theoretical but as a holistic approach to ways of thinking and doing things. For with the emergence of the printed book and the subsequent victory of humanism, the ideal division of the world in a theoretical and a practical sphere took command. It was Leon Battista Alberti who first established this division in architecture by splitting up architectural practice in design and artisanship—giving *disegno* a clear primacy. According to Alberti, architects are responsible for the design, in contrast to the craftsman who is responsible for the execution of the building according to the architect's plans—thereby differentiating something which had been unified before. This divide has initiated a fundamental shift in the identity of architecture as an art system. In this context, Nelson Goodman's notation theory is helpful to describe this shift as one that altered architecture's character from an autographic to an allographic art. Goodman distinguishes between an autographic notation system like paintings, where the material instantiation and the work are one and the same, whereas in an allographic system, e.g., music or theater performances, the work and its instantiations are not one and the same. In this sense, architecture has become a notational problem.

Today, we are facing a media revolution that is equal to the upheaval of the invention of the printing press.
Curiously, the digital tools provided by CAD and CAM seem to induce a reversal of the divide between design and production described above. One of the main reasons for this development is the reintroduction of a continuous process implying designing as well as manufacturing; a process that is controlled by the computing technology. This seamless and

interactive process changes again our way of making things. Is this the "double murder" effect mentioned above? And if so, in which state would architecture resurrect itself from death?

José Salinas's installation *Disembodiment*, which was produced for Isolde Nagel's A trans Pavilion in Berlin, might lead us toward an answer to this question.[4] In this work, Salinas deals with the relationship between the way we move through the city and the effects that the built environment has upon our body. Ambient design would be too weak a term to describe this work, and to fully understand the approach. The installation reveals a much deeper question that involves the notion of the body in the digital age. It is not only interesting but also paradigmatic that José Salinas has chosen to use the human body as the working field of his experiments since 2004. But why are we so obsessed with the body, especially since we thought that the digital age would lead us to a "disembodiment," as the title of the installation also suggests. José Salinas is interested in the feedback between the environment and the body, as purported in a famous phrase by Winston Churchill: "First we shape our buildings; thereafter they shape us." What kind of affective relation could there be between the environment and our body? Currently, we can observe a genuine renaissance of the affective, i.e., of the notion of the body, not only within architecture but also as a general social trend.[5] In the arts, in cultural studies, in the media, and even in the sciences, the investigation of affects plays a major role. This "affective turn" reflects

our desire to gain an elemental access to the world via aesthetic perception. In the field of architecture, the interest has shifted accordingly to architecture's capability to produce effects that in turn produce affects in an immediate fashion. Obviously, this approach implies a wide range of architectural means: material effects, bodily perception, tactility, ambience, sensuality, and sensibility. In the end, these means would create an environment in which the body could immerse.

According to German philosopher Peter Sloterdijk, "architecture is before anything else the design of immersion." For him, to build houses is a problem of love, because architecture is a place where we must open ourselves totally and surrender: "The totalitarianism of architecture is a totalitarianism of love, a love of space, an entrancement, not by something that is vis-à-vis us, but instead by something that envelops us like a shell or a skin." This topophilic feeling is a precondition that allows us to immerse in built environments. Immersion, then, is a technique for relinquishing our bodily boundaries, and "a de-framing procedure for images and perspectives."[6]

"But what happens when images are no longer perceived as being separate from our own bodies, when we are instead drawn into images?" This question, raised by cultural scientist Marie-Louise Angerer, points to the core of the problem. What happens "when these images evade the representative level and act directly upon the pre-linguistic body?" It is precisely here that the concept of affect

4 Cf. José Salinas's installation *Disembodiment* at A trans Pavilion, Berlin. March 8–May 3, 2008. Curated by Isolde Nagel
5 Marie-Louise Angerer, "Affekt und Begehren oder: Was macht den Affekt so begehrenswert?," in the e-journal *Philosophie der Psychologie*, http://www.jp.philo.at/texte/AngererM1.pdf. January 2006
6 Peter Sloterdijk, "Immersion," in: *ARCH+* 178. June 2006, pp. 58–59

applies and "the affective body as the 'framer' of no longer framed pictures is especially in demand." If we understand our built and digital environments as "de-framing procedures" that produce immersive environments, then we can understand our obsession with the body. In the end we are dependent upon the body as a frame, as an instrument of perception. Paradoxically, it was the new media and the much-attested digital revolution that have introduced this "affective turn." According to Mark B. Hansen, a cultural theoretician, "the technical expansion of self-affection allows for a fuller and more intense experience of subjectivity."[7] The new technical developments have enabled us to experience subjectivity in the most radical manner. For in fact, it was the digital revolution that heralded the turn from language to affect and feeling. From the very beginning, key issues of the digital discourse have been tactile sensations, instantaneity, immediacy, and the dissolution of time and space. According to Angerer, we have come a long way to bring theory and practice together again: "Wonderful times were yet to come, because we could finally bid farewell to all of

these post-structural thinkers: their theories, that is to say, would now confront us in incarnate form in the network."[8]

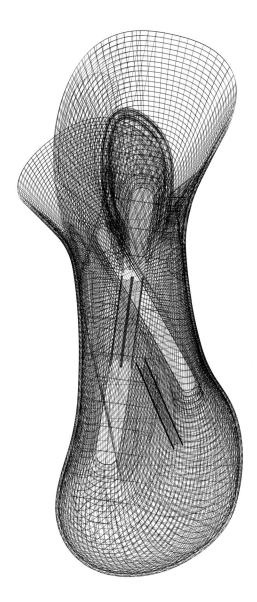

7 Cf. Mark B. Hansen, "The Time of Affect, or Bearing Witness to Life," in: *Critical Inquiry*, Vol. 30, No. 3. Spring 2005
8 Cf. Marie-Louise Angerer, p. 2

1
Revisiting: The Line as Form of Expression

Artists and architects visualize their thoughts and ideas through drawing (analog, digital), and it is the line as a form of expression that helps us to render our thinking processes. Throughout history, the line has been, without doubt, the main stream for representing space. Therefore, it seems interesting enough to revisit the primary conditions of the line and analyze if new conditions have appeared, and if so, to understand their transformations and variations. Since the Renaissance, new drawing techniques and tools for representing space have been implemented in the drawing process, which is a format capable of rendering and measuring space; there has always been the need to find ways of bringing our thoughts to the surface and presenting them in an understandable format. Through time, the techniques evolved and consistently developed new methods. At this point, I want to consider a period of time where lots of changes occured very rapidly—the beginning of the twentieth century. I will recall *Pedagogical Sketchbook* (1925) by Paul Klee, and *Point and Line to Plane* (1925) by Wassily Kandinsky, published by Sibyl Moholy-Nagy and Walter Gropius as part of the fourteen Bauhaus Books. These books were conceived as statements of the artists' methodologies, from a theoretical and practical point of view. The students could understand the differences in their artistic processes as well as the avant-garde art, even though contemporary art expressions were so different and looked very confusing and difficult from a more academic art stream. Indeed, those artistic processes had very specific and conscious analytical statements behind them. They were all looking at nature from a different point of view, as a resource for introspective search that could lead to a creative process. Indeed, nature was the main resource for inspiration, as the exchange and contact with other disciplines was very limited or did not exist. However, in the last decades, architecture has been looking into other disciplines for exchange of ideas, techniques, tools, and new modes of representation. Therefore, architecture has changed quite dramatically by incorporating the computer in the design process. Indeed, the computer was a new tool which allowed the development of new conceptual approaches and techniques.

Therefore, academic institutions changed their academic programs to accommodate the theoretical and technical changes that the new tools brought to the field of architecture.

However, it appears there is still a gap to be filled. There is a very important disjunction between theoretical approaches and the conceptualized proposal. The fact that now we have more and more sophisticated computers, equipped with highly sophisticated and capable applications and software, does not guarantee that the conceived proposal is a contemporary design. Complexity and funky forms generated by computers means nothing in this context. Architecture without a conceptualization process is just a funky image of an object. The contents of this book will focus on the understanding of the different processes that appear after releasing the abstract line isolated from the objective environment of the material form into specific external conditions. Indeed, new tools offer new possibilities, but also carry other considerations such as deeper questioning and conceptualization processes. Therefore, on one hand we have to master the tool, on the other hand, we have to develop a working method. Furthermore, the first step we have to take is to start rethinking the line, if we want to develop a consistent contemporary design process. The line does not mean the same in the nineteenth, twentieth, or indeed, the twenty-first century.

While we are working with lines, we understand lines as forms of expression that connect, extend, and/or detect continuities (even sometimes invisible and unperceived) within a field of influence. Indeed, depending on the scale depicted, the line undertakes a radical form of abstraction through a multilinear remapping of complex existing conditions, and filtering multilayered information recorded from our observa-

tions and thoughts. The line's initial ambition is to reconnect, establishing a continuum within the discontinuity of the processes. However, in the process of reconnecting all relationships are reassessed, both new and pre-existing. Instead of treating the lines as external support, the line strategy sets up a network of potential spatial and programming connections, both internally and with existing conditions. The lines mapped become medial, or translational: the line seeks to mediate between otherwise competing programs, refusing strategies that effectively generate isolation and confinement. Furthermore, the line strategy depicts existing conditions as a direct abstraction and extension of the potential relationships encountered in the process of transition. Indeed, the result of this strategy is most evident where multilinear conditions and spatial conditions merge into one seamless diagram. Historically, an important part of the analog strategies pursued in the development of the design process includes physical diagrams made less as representations of a proposed building strategy, and more as forms of material computation of the forces that can be seen as organizational diagrams for the desired proposal. These physical diagrams depict the operations of bending, twisting, and deformation of three-dimensional (3D) multilinear paths, which in turn have the potential to become a diagrammatic design tool for organizing the existing conditions (a material modeling approach to form-finding that was pioneered in the 1960s experiments of Frei Otto and his colleagues at the Institute for Lightweight Structures in Stuttgart).

Constructed with inputs that correspond to the existing conditions, these physical diagrams were then allowed to physically adapt themselves as a consequence of the various forces applied to the configured digital methodologies. The line-diagrams created by these "performative" physical diagrams closely resemble the smooth and curvilinear conditions extracted from the existing. Information from the physical diagrams is then passed into digital tools that will determine the most appropriate digital methodology. Digital methodologies have been implemented extensively in various disciplines of contemporary non-linear mathematics. We are always looking at different disciplines' working processes, and we found in the dynamics of path formation and complex behaviors–analogies to be incorporated in the design process as means of dynamic strategies capable of assimilating unanticipated changes in program, use, and occupancy over time. Researchers from different disciplines have integrated their work on crowd motion in a model of aggregate motion and change, depicting a balance between opposing sets of forces, showing that the whole system is affected by how decisions are made. Furthermore, they simulated their models of existing conditions as a physical performative field, which effectively allows the location of multilinear conditions by computing various alternative formal organizational patterns. Indeed, there is a continuous multidirectional shifting loop between analog strategies and digital methodologies. In this book, there is a very important interest in treating the lines as a means for mediating movements between scales that will make the lines operative at different scales simultaneously. Therefore, the line asserts the need to see shifting and transition processes as gradual and evolutionary. Indeed, in order to let shifting and transition processes emerge, there must be certain properties embedded in the line. If we constrain ourselves to R3, there are many important properties embedded in the line, but above all inflection is the ideal genetic element of the variable line.

Inflection is the elastic point, the genetic element of the active, spontaneous line. For Bernard Cache, inflection–or point of inflection–is an intrinsic singularity. If we look at other disciplines, we will find that they look at the same aspect that we are looking at, from a different point of view. Indeed, if mathematics were to look at inflection, they could find that the most interesting aspect of inflection is its capacity for variation. Then it will assume variation as its objective, and the notion of function tends to be extracted, but the notion of objective also changes and becomes functional. Indeed, the implementation of the notion of continuous variation in the design process has been a critical aspect in the development of our design methodologies, which goes beyond traditional Euclidean geometry and Cartesian grid organizational systems. It implies the incorporation of non-Euclidean geometry in our design process and as an extension of the generation of non-linear geometry systems. In some important mathematical writings, Leibniz posits the idea of dynamic strategies able to assimilate unanticipated changes in program, use, and occupancy over time. "Architects could not use the fourth dimension or hyperbolic space in the same instrumental way in which they used triangles or projections, but they could allude to them, and that is what they did."[1]

Therefore, while scientific and mathematical inquiries are now at its heart, deeply optimistic and seeking the fullness of their respective disciplines, architecture found deep complications. Architecture was and is still unable to accept them. In architecture, the questions lie not only in the usefulness of a particular understanding of space, but also in the interpretation of the manifestations of a particular method. Indeed, it is up to us to determine our own

1 Robin Evans *The Projective Cast: Architecture and Its Three Geometries*. MIT Press Cambridge,1995

method and evaluate its manifestations. For this, it is crucial to imply systematic operations, in order to set up the specific movement from line to surface that we are seeking. Architecture traditionally understands the straight line as a degree two component ($y=ax+b$, $y'=dy/dx=a$), because of the restrictions of Cartesian space. However, advanced 3D softwares are designed by mathematicians and software engineers who consider the line as a degree three component ($y'=dy/dx=cx+d$, $y''=c$). Therefore, they understand line and topology (surface) as components with the same degree three. Within this plane of immanence, the line could become a surface (topology), and the topology could become a line.

Once we have analyzed the line's embedded properties, we can analyze that the line—by affiliation with others—extends and could exchange its properties with others; and vice versa. By extension, the line will be establishing a fibris of lines which will become the organizational system of potential surfaces that they will configure. The organizational lines system should be understood as a topology, which is a system of geometric properties that remain invariant under certain variations, transformations, and/or mutations; a collection of open sets making a given set a topological space. Therefore, it is critical to determine the topological organizational line system, which will remain invariant and will be the base for developing the systematic consistency we are seeking for the design process. This is the keynote for the movement, transition from line to topology.

Once we have determined the topology we want to work with, it is very important to configure a set of operations on the topology, so that we can conduct an evaluation. Thus, I will mention some operations that could be applied to the topology, in order to generate a design methodology:

1.*Manifold*: generalization of N-dimensional space in which a neighborhood of each point, called its chart, looks like Euclidean space. The charts are related to each other by Cartesian coordinate transformations and comprise an atlas for the manifold. The atlas may be non-trivially connected; there are round-trip tours of a manifold that cannot be contracted to a point. The surface of a donut, called a torus, is a familiar non-trivial 2D manifold.

2.*Submanifold, ambient space*: a submanifold is a subset of a manifold, its ambient space, for which each point has a chart in which the submanifold looks like a linear subspace of lower dimension. A common knot is a one-dimensional ambient space.

3.*Homotopy*: a continuous deformation of a mathematical object which preserves its topological integrity but may develop self-intersections and even worse singularities. There is a homotopy that turns a teapot into a torus (a sphere with a hole). There is another deforming it into a point.

4.*Isotopy*: a homotopy of an object produced by a deformation of the ambient space, so there the object cannot develop new self-intersections. The deformation of the teapot to a torus is an isotopy, but the deformaton to a point is not.

5.*Embedding*: the parameterization of a submanifold by means of a standard model. A knotted sphere in four-space is an embedding of the familiar round sphere. Whitney's theorem says that an N-dimensional manifold is guaranteed to have an embedding in Euclidean 2N-space.

6.*Immersion*: a locally (but not globally) smoothly invertible mapping of one manifold into another.

The image may have self-intersections.

7.*Minimal Surface*: a surface that locally has the smallest area given a particular topological shape for it, and possibly, constrained by a fixed boundary or prescribed behavior at infinity.

8.*Steepest Descent Method*: a particular way of guiding an isotopy of an embedded surface to one that minimizes a function that measures its shape. Moving down the gradient of the area function often terminates at a minimal surface (Munzner, http://www.geom.uiuc.edu/docs/research/ieee94/node8.html).

In order to implement these operations on the topology, it is necessary to systematize and to configure relations between System–Process–Methodology–Tools–Production, so the assemblage will reach conceptual clarity and precision. Indeed, the systematic configuration between System–Process–Methodology–Tools–Production should be as flexible and malleable as possible. However, I would like to emphasize that it is not a linear process, but rather non-linear and multilinear. This *modus operandi* no longer refers its condition to a spatial relation method-form, but to a temporal modulation that implies the continuous variation of form as a continuous development of method. Therefore, we could affirm that this temporal continuous variation is what Leibniz is defining when stating that the law of series posits curves as "the traces of the same line" in a continuous movement. It is not only a temporal but also a qualitative conception of the object. The object becomes an event. The object is the reflection of the stage of all actions acting on the topology. It is the momentum of equilibrium brought to maximum expression between the operations and the topology.

Urban Field: complex interactivity of existing network conditions in relationship to nodal urban infrastructural agglomerations

Critical Nodes: programmatic relationship+existing conditions. Richness of difference

Revisiting: The Line as Form of Expression

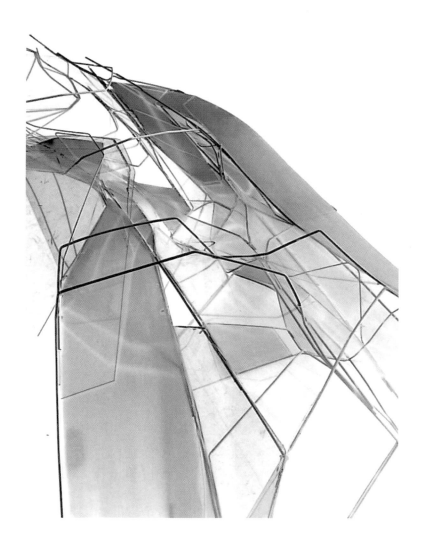

Furnishing Field: structural principles+occupancy

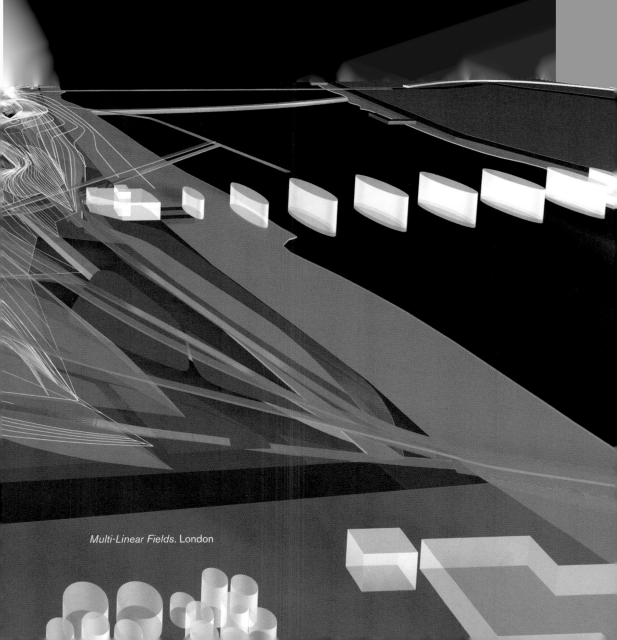

Multi-Linear Fields. London

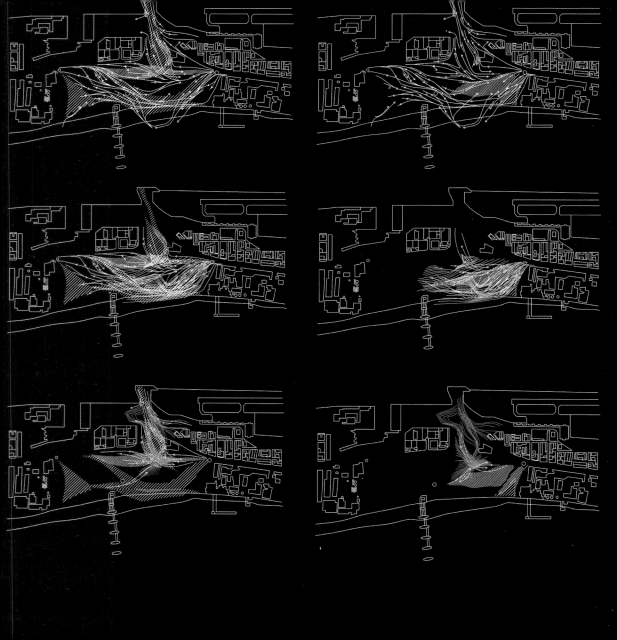

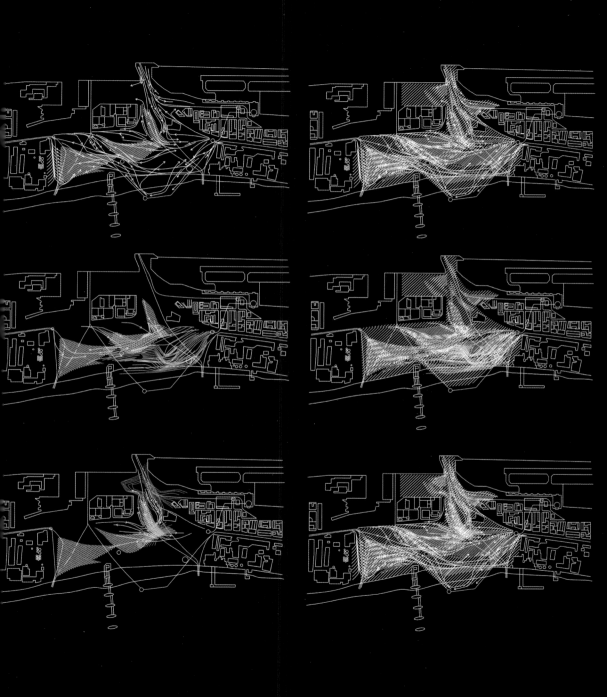

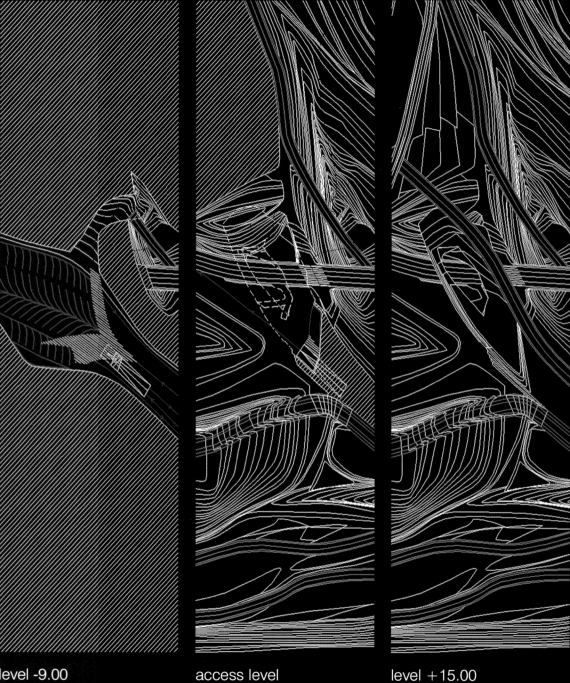

level -9.00   access level   level +15.00

parking & car mov.
pedestrian paths

infrastructure
DRL rail

intersection effect
high permanence

chain + local pattern
fat
temporal

structural layout

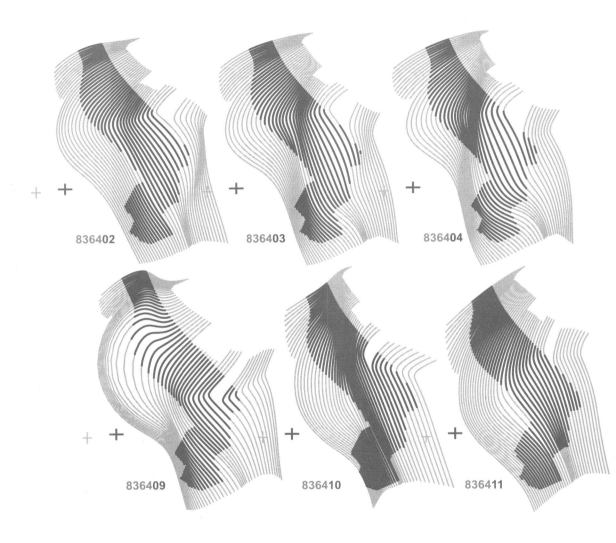

836402

836403

836404

836409

836410

836411

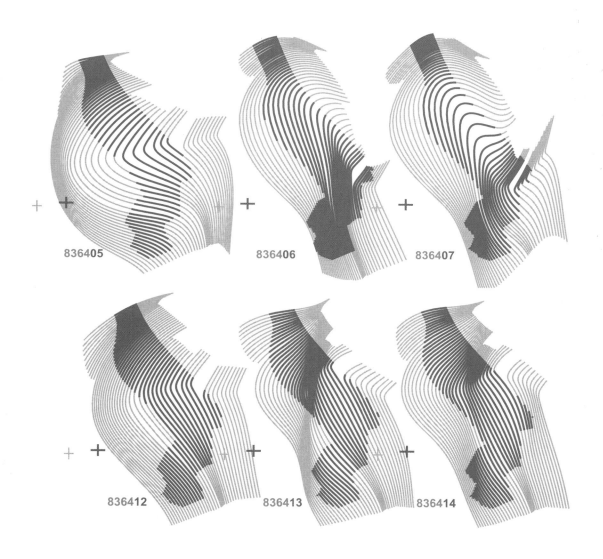

836405

836406

836407

836412

836413

836414

Tono Sci-Research City. Japan

31

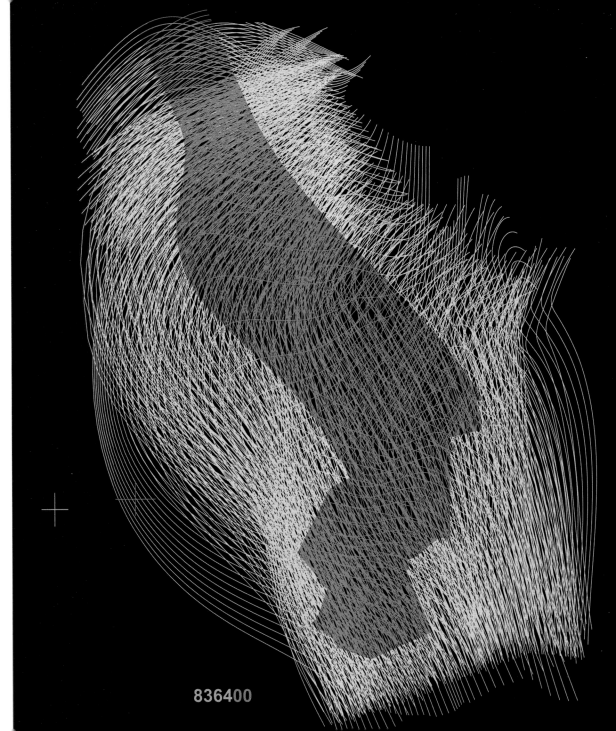

836400

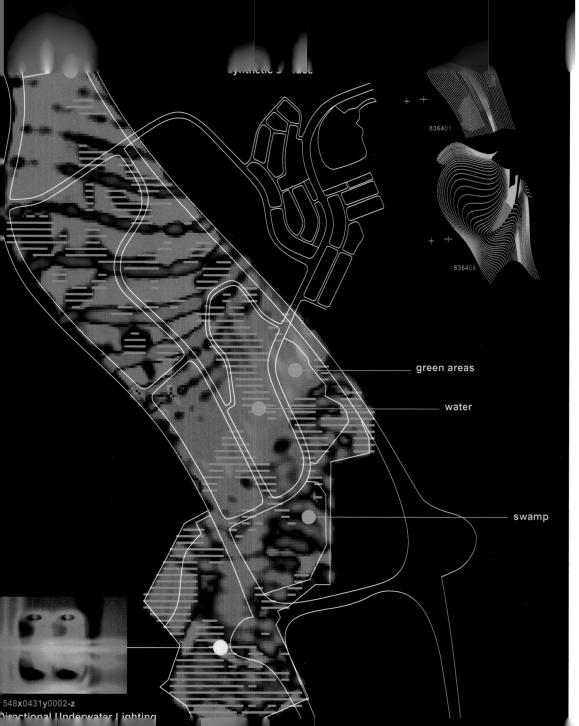

Synthetic Surface

836401

836408

green areas

water

swamp

548x0431y0002-z

Directional Underwater Lighting

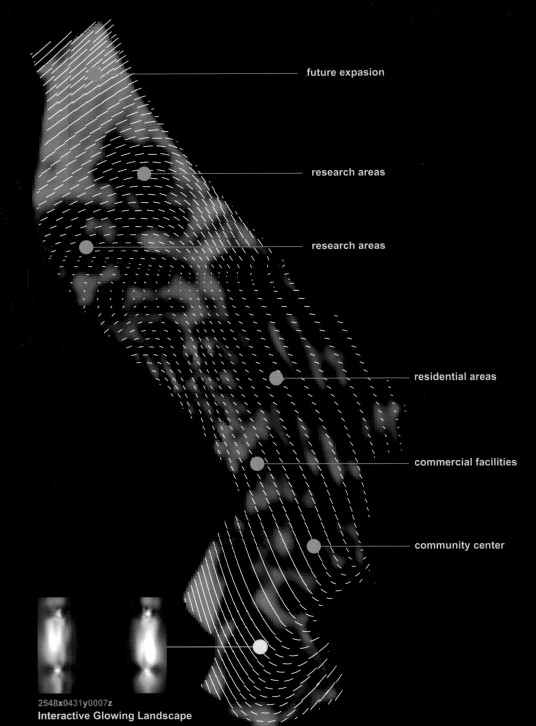

future expasion

research areas

research areas

residential areas

commercial facilities

community center

2548x0431y0007z
Interactive Glowing Landscape

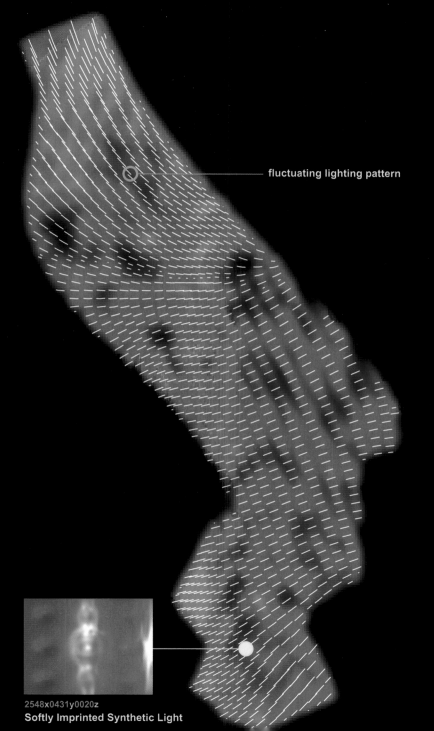

fluctuating lighting pattern

2548x0431y0020z
Softly Imprinted Synthetic Light

2
Diagram to Proposal

Lines and diagrams would seem to be distinct. The line retains its identity, whilst at the same time it operates within the diagram. This is not to suggest that line and diagram are not different but rather that the ground of the difference is the pervasive sameness enjoined by representation. Evidence of that sameness is the identification of what is taken to be a relatively unproblematic move from modes of representation to proposal. Therefore, it is only with the enforcer abeyance of representation—understood as that which determines their field of operation—that the real particularity of the diagram and the line would then be able to emerge. The important point is not simply the problematic status of representation within architecture, but that allowing representation centrality precludes any real consideration being given to the diagram as a field of experimentation. Allowing for this identification of the specific will take place in this instance in terms of tracing the consequences for the line and diagram once the possibility of experimentation is introduced. Therefore, a beginning can be made by allowing the retained centrality representation to confront the possibility of experimentation.

At this point we could ask: is there a link between the line and the diagram, and the possibility of experimentation? The immediate answer must be that there is not. Lines and diagrams, once they are assumed to represent, cannot sustain experimentation on their own terms. By definition, a representation always refers to what it represents. What this formulation entails is that lines and diagrams are held within a relation where their identity and status is determined by what they are not. Moreover, the instantiation of what they represent needs to be understood as a form of completion, therefore, experimentation is precluded.

When a line or a diagram becomes experimental ground, then they can no longer be understood as representations since they would have given up that determining hold in which identity is determined by a relation to an outside. Consequently, answering the question concerning the possible relation between lines, diagrams, and experimentation in the affirmative, necessitates a reformulation of the line and the diagram in order to determine experimentation. In place of the complete, there has to be the incomplete. The latter is not the negation of completion. In fact another type of completion has to emerge. The incomplete signals the possibility of the continual reworking and opening up of lines or diagrams. The presence of the space of experimentation arises when neither is taken as complete in itself. Rather, it is the inscription of the reality of a productive negativity within the field opened by both the line and the diagram that complete and incomplete will evolve and open up a potential ground of experimentation.

The line already marks a space, marks it out by dividing and creating space. The diagram does not hold to the spatial possibilities of something other than itself. Nor, for that matter, do lines and diagrams exist as ends in themselves. However, the history of the line as representing, as standing for, and thus as acting out, is there at the posited origin of painting. The drawing of the line as the origin of painting links the line to the work of representation. A common representation example is the perspective as a representational technique to visualize space, where the line is the element that organizes the system of proportions/dimensions on the flat canvas. However, there are some artists whose intention of challenging line-drawing conventions took them to redefine the condition of the line.

Jackson Pollock's lines are not representational, but rather shifting networked fields that act as haptic spaces of lines. In addition, the unconventional understanding of the lines opens up ways to challenge more common interpretations of the line and develop operative lines that will allow generative diagrams. However, we should not see representation as an end in itself, but as an end of "possibilities" that could offer a more detailed perspective in terms of oppositions. Therefore, representation will define opening in terms of closure, which refers to the demands made by the incorporation of the line or diagram into the structure of representation. Within that structure, a line defines both itself and what it is not.

A diagram envisages an instantiation in which the envisaged object is what the diagram is taken to represent. While absence predominates, the closure is still posited insofar as the line now tracing and marking the absent figure presents that figure and thus allows for its re-identification and reconfiguration. Openings and closures are inter-articulated with the enforcing work of absence. Fundamental to this formulation is the interrelation between absence and its overcoming. What this interrelation allows, however, is a distinction between two different conceptions of absence. In the first place, there would be absence and its overcoming as marking the work of representation; representation as re-presentation, signaling both the presence of absence and its envisioned overcoming. On the other hand, there is another sense of absence which would refer to the incomplete. Within architecture the instantiation of the incomplete could then be thought of in terms of Bataille's conception of the l'informe. Working within the structure of representation, the openings at work in representation's formulation occur in different contexts. Representation is always more complex than a simple oscillation between presence and absence. Each context involves the effective presence of a specific type of opposition. The oppositions presence/absence, model/real object, plan/building, for example, instantiate a specific desire and thus specific forms of operation. The desire is the possibility that one side of the opposition holds and presents what the other side either is or will be. At the origin of painting, the image of the one who is absent has to be the actual likeness of the absent one. The image has to stand for that which is not there. It has to present it and therefore the image has to be its re-presentation. In the case of the model/real object opposition, the model will have to have become the real object. The plan becomes the building. Plan and model stand for what is absent, but only on the condition that presence is possible. The dictates of representation are such that movement across the divide defines activity. Moreover, it defines the way either side of the painting is to be interpreted. In other words, it is not just that representation determines the way the line, plan, or diagram is to be understood, it also demands that the completed object be assembled as their instantiation. The question that each opening poses concerns how the divide is to be crossed; how is the opening to be closed? Once the line or diagram is given with the structure of representation, then this question is inexorably present. It presents that version of the incomplete that is determined by the need for completion. Therefore, this sense of the incomplete cannot be located outside the object. The space given by the movement of completion—the movement between diagram and building for example—no longer provides the site of the incomplete. Once taken as internal to the object—the object as already complete and thus completed with the possible internal inscription of the incomplete—the incomplete can be understood as part of the building's economy. Nonetheless, responding to the demand for closure is to turn the plan, drawing, model, or the line into that which can only be explained within the structure of representation. It should not be forgotten that this structure allows for its own negative instance; namely a series of drawing, models, plans, et cetera whose interest is determined by the claim that they have purely presentational force. They could, for example, be taken as either fantastic possibilities or utopian projections. Gesturing to the impossibility of the realization of the desire for completion, they become representation's negative instance. Impos-

sibility, within this formulation, is no more than the negative instance of possibility. What this means is that the possibility of retrieving the line, of allowing the diagram another possibility, is not to be interpreted within the terms set by representation's positive or negative dimensions. Representation stages its own limits. In order to chart them, it is of fundamental importance to allow representation to dictate both positive and negative instances. The reason for this importance is linked to the description, already given, of the divide that has to be crossed and which forms, from within the interpretive purview of representation, an integral part of an account of either plan, drawing, or diagram. A plan reveals what is going to be present. What this means is that representation dictates that the plan or the diagram hold that absent presence in place. There is, therefore, a certain futurity inscribed in the existence of the plan or diagram.

Consequently, the future is not a condition of the present, such that the future could have been inscribed in that which is present. Rather, the future is opened, demanded, because of a lack necessitating an envisioned completion that characterizes the presence. It is precisely this particular determination that is at work in the suggestion that the origin of painting is linked to the outline of that which is necessarily absent. What is of primary concern is the opening and hence the link between line, drawing, and diagram and a pervading sense of absence. What absence signals is the interpretive demand. What that means in this context is that the site of interpretation is marked by what it is not. This quality—the "what it is not"—needs to be linked to the future. The "what it is not" is connected to the "what it will be." This definition of the context has a number of interrelated consequences. There are two that are critical. The first concerns the particularity of the line, drawing, plan, etc. The subsequent building reinforces the ascription of loss. The second consequence refers to the way either the line or the diagram is to be interpreted. These two consequences are related insofar as what arises with the second are the results of definitions that involve no more than simple negations. However, it has to be a conception of becoming that holds the movement to form. There cannot be pure process without that movement. With mere becoming, form is precluded and therefore the architectural is continually deferred. Allowing form as inter-articulated with movement and, therefore, with the centrality of becoming is the potential within Leibniz's theory of the monad. The distance being staged here is from a structure in which there is an envisioned movement from the presentation of "what is yet to be"—thereby defining that presentation as the representation of "what it is not"—to the subsequent realization of that earlier representation. What this means is that given the demands of this structure the "yet to be" comes to be completed. Allusion has already been made to this conception in terms of the "what it is not." Within this formulation, the diagram and the line are what they are because they allow for a completion in a time that is not their own. Having been completed—completed in the sense of having been instantiated—both the line and the diagram are necessarily devoid of possibilities. Therefore, they lose their capacity for investigation or research. This does not just mean that the possibility for experimentation is linked to the incomplete, but that experimentation needs to allow what had been taken to be representations to sustain a generative quality and therefore, to allow interpretations beyond the hold of representation—moving as it must from the incomplete

to the complete and thus from the present to the future; this quality is denied because lines, diagrams, and plans are taken as demanding their own completion and thus of having been completed. What predominates here is a conception of negation that is linked to its own overcoming through the act of completion (either real or envisioned). Neither the truth nor the viability of this setup comprise what is central to this position. Centrality has to be given to the demand for the act of completion. Realization precludes experimentation precisely because it is the mark of this act of completion, or at least that is the demand that is made. There is a twofold movement at work here. Representation denies that either the line or the diagram could present possibilities resisting completion. Moreover, to the extent that either were allowed to have this capacity, then neither the line nor the diagram could be interpreted within the determinations given by the work of representation. How then does it become possible to account for the work of lines and the field of activity given by the diagram? What this means is that rather than open out by trying to stand for what they are not, the line and diagram open up within themselves. Allowing for the continuity of this opening, allowing for the continuity of an opening resisting absolute finality and thus an enforcing completion, is to allow for both line and diagram to take on the status of plural events. Plurality here does not refer to the domain of meaning where plurality would be mere semantic overdetermination. Rather, for the diagram or the line to take on this status they would become the site of an ontological irreducibility. They would, for example, articulate the determinations of the Leibnizian monad once its demands were drawn. Moreover, it is in terms of the monad that representation as an effect can be reintroduced. The monad allows for representation precisely because it is not formulated and articulated within a structure of representation. For Leibniz, within the general structure of argument presented in *The Monadology*, the monad always presents itself and can be perceived as such in a particular form at a particular time. Nonetheless, the monad is always more than this formal actuality. And yet the "more" is not derived from links to the monad. On the contrary, it is internal to the monad itself. Leibniz formulates this in terms of the "principle of change" being internal to the monad. The monad is in its continual opening up within itself. It could not be described as the continuity of an opening without end unless there was the fundamental recognition that the monad is, at the very same time, an endless opening always having a particular form. The monad is the co-presence of continuity and discontinuity; of form and the generation of form; of instantiation and becoming. A production of endless completion opened by the effective presence of the incomplete—it allows the monad to become the diagram. While it would necessitate a more sustained engagement with Leibniz that can be developed here, what has to be taken up are the possibilities inherent in the formulation of the monad as "multiplicity in unity." With this movement, one that in general terms is occasioned by the diagram having the ontological status of a plural event, it becomes the site of experimentation. The diagram is the place of a mapping and remapping in which finitude is always an effect of an ineliminable infinite. In part, what this means can only be understood once it is recognized that the diagram and the line are not the representation of "multiplicity in unity." The diagram cannot be taken as re-presenting this setup. Quite simply, there cannot be a re-presentation of complex relations where complexity involves both onto-

logical and temporal considerations. They can only be enacted. The diagram, in order to maintain itself as the site of experimentation, has to work with that possibility. When Leibniz refers to the "infinite folds of the soul," it is not as though there could have been an accompanying drawing detailing that infinity. The infinite in that instance involves the demand to think the relationship between the finite and the infinite, such that a cross-section would map that relation. The monad, once formulated in terms of a founding and ineliminable plurality (therefore as plural events), raise the question of their own presentation.

Reading the diagram as a plural event, therefore, is not to read it as a monad, or even as a site containing the soul's "infinite folds," since such an approach would be too literal.

Experimentation, understood as the opening freedom at work—once the hold of representation—is the co-presence of the complete and the incomplete. It is not as though there is a representation of that relation. This complex process of possible and actual interrelations sets the conditions within which lines and diagrams are to be read. What is read, therefore, is the line at work. The pragmatic occurrence is the possibility of a reintroduction of representation. It can occur in two ways. The first occurs in an act of re-reading. What defines the act is the interpretive refusal to read that which was taken to be simply representational as a mere representation. The second is more productive and more closely linked to the question of experimentation. While it can be argued that the diagram as presented above is not itself a re-presentation in the strict sense of the term, this does not preclude the possibility that at certain points or at certain moments, elements of the diagram can be attributed a representational quality.

Such an attribution would be pragmatic and strategic. As such, representation and thus the capacity to represent, become effects of the diagram rather than the diagram's architectural extension. In addition, freeing the diagram from the hold of representation, but allowing re-presentation to be present as a possible effect, opens up both a theoretical question, as well as an architectural one. How is the movement from the line to the diagram, and by extension, from diagram to proposal, to be conceived and therefore enacted? Once the diagram is attri-buted a different status, then areas of inquiry— and indeed areas of experimentation—emerge as given within the gap between diagram and proposal. In conclusion, we could remark upon the need for setting the work of lines and dia-grams within the possibility of experimentation within architecture. In this first instance, once freed from the need to represent, the line and the diagram work as ends in themselves. This is not intended to preclude pragmatic neces-sities; rather, it is to allow for the emergence of the diagram as plotting a complexity of relations that it is always more than the additions of elements.

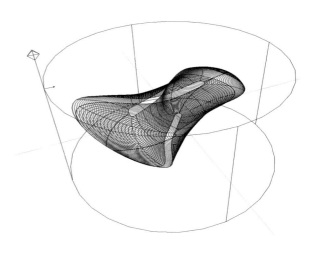

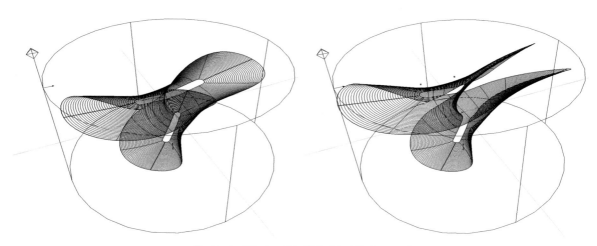

Topological Body within Cylindrical Environment

41

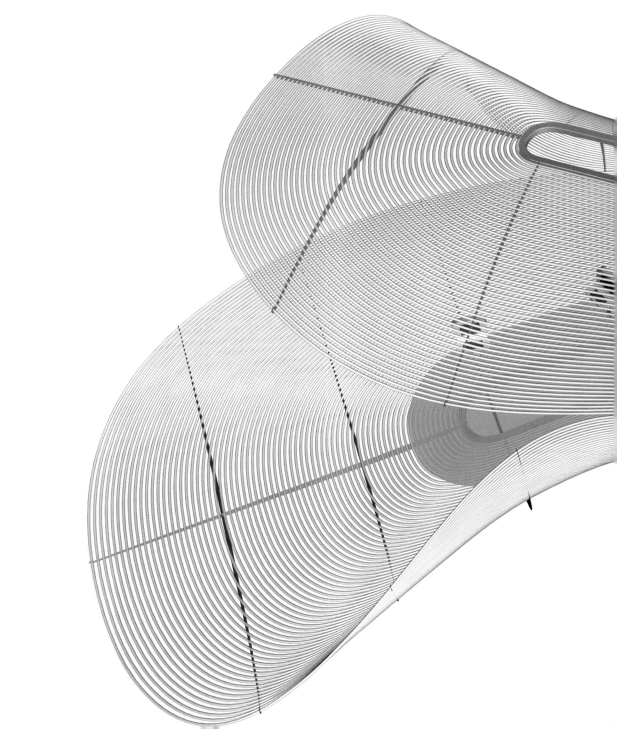

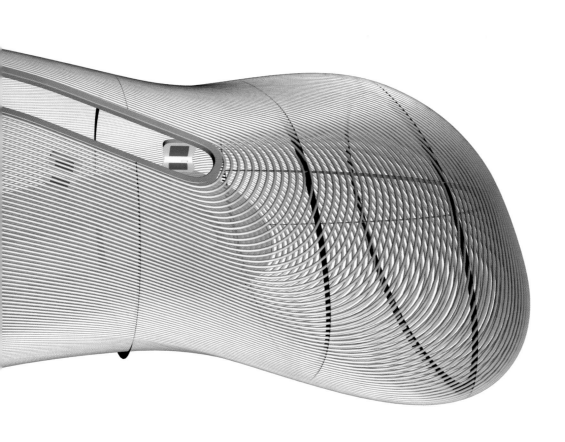

Intelligent Surface: Multimedia Platform for 2004 Olympic Games. Greece

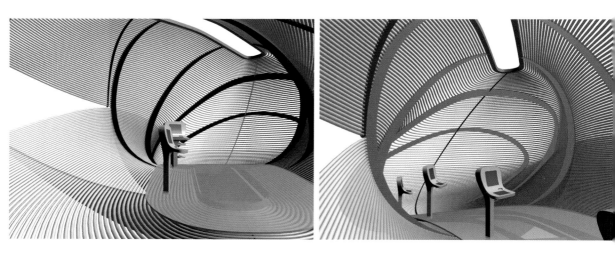

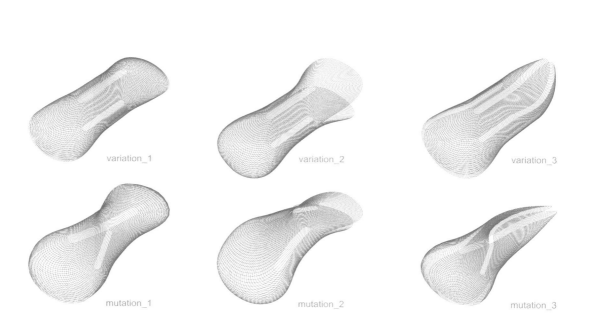

variation_1

variation_2

variation_3

mutation_1

mutation_2

mutation_3

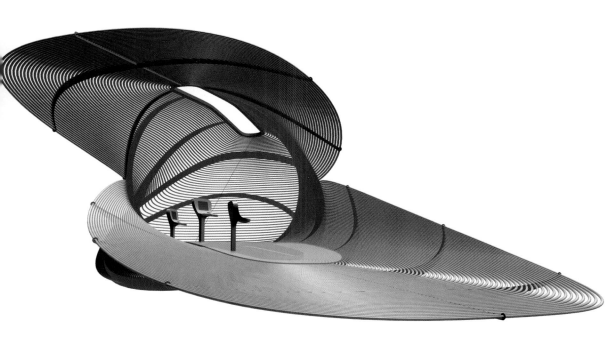

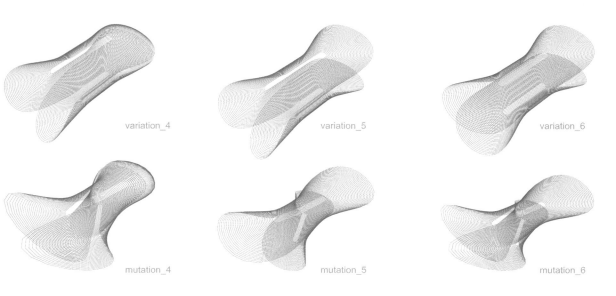

variation_4

variation_5

variation_6

mutation_4

mutation_5

mutation_6

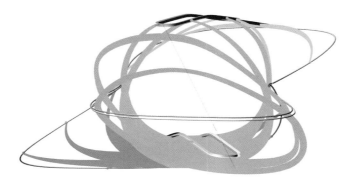

back structural rings elevation

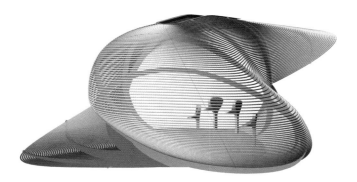

back elevation

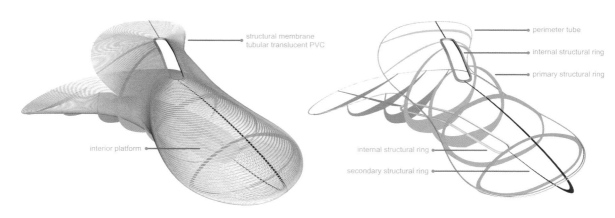

structural membrane
tubular translucent PVC

interior platform

perimeter tube

internal structural ring

primary structural ring

internal structural ring

secondary structural ring

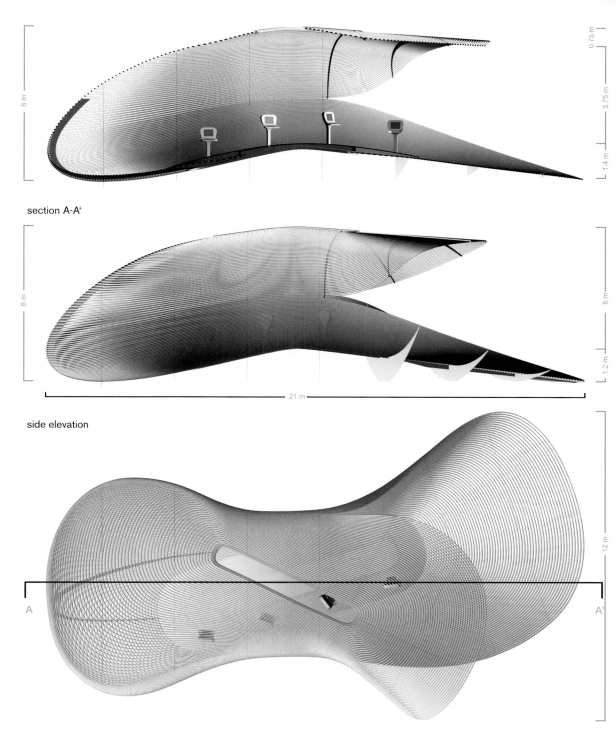

section A-A'

side elevation

6 m

0.75 m

3.75 m

1.4 m

6 m

6 m

1.2 m

21 m

12 m

A

A'

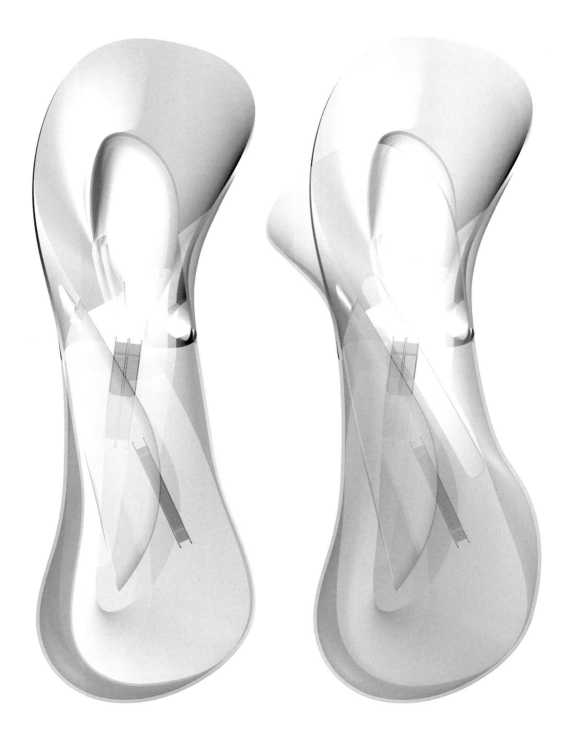

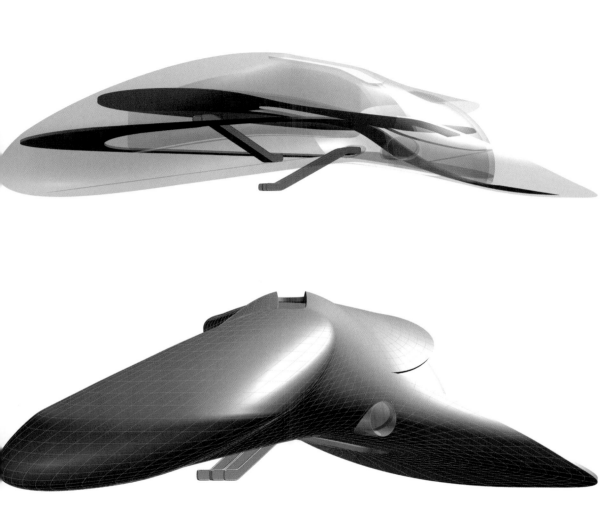

Museum in TL-SYNC. South Korea

rot 000 000 006

rot 000 000 018

rot 000 000 198

rot 000 000 015

rot 000 000 036

rot 000 000 216

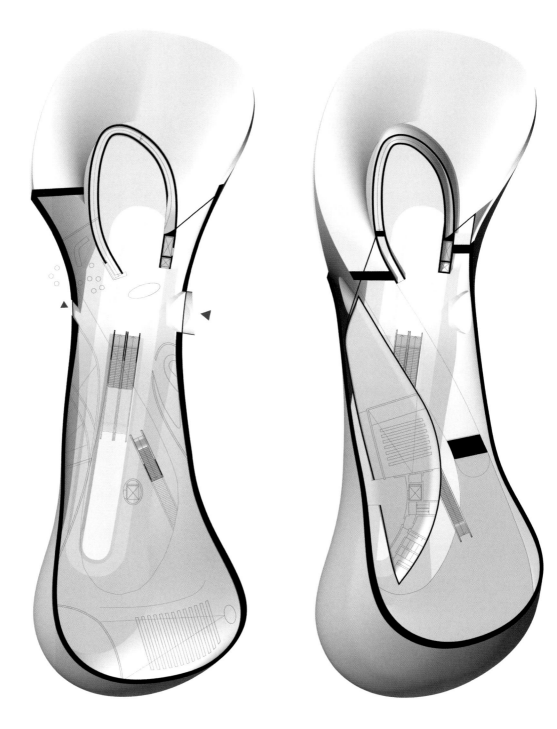

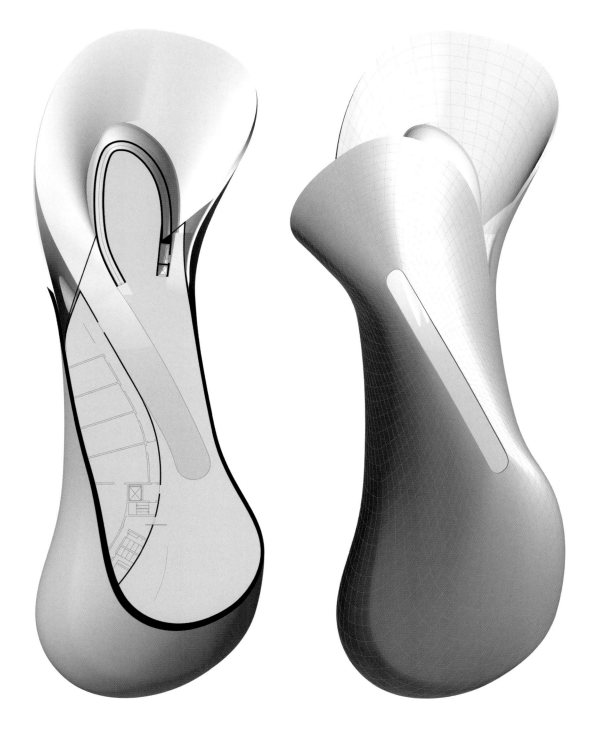

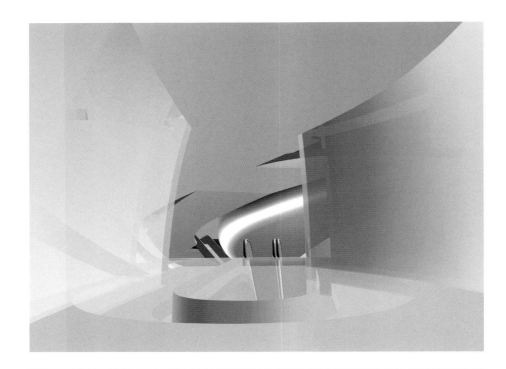
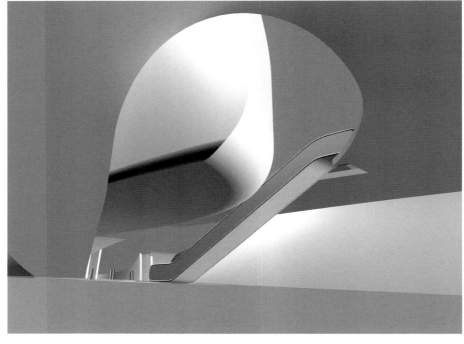

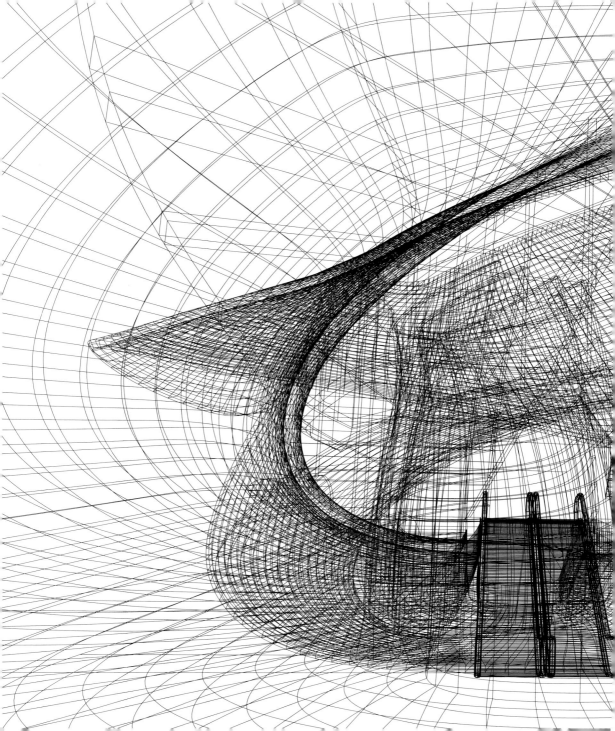

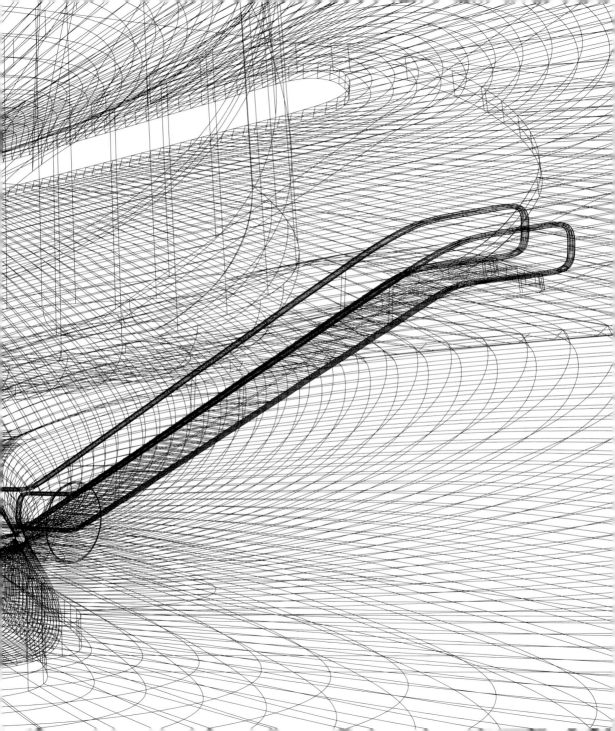

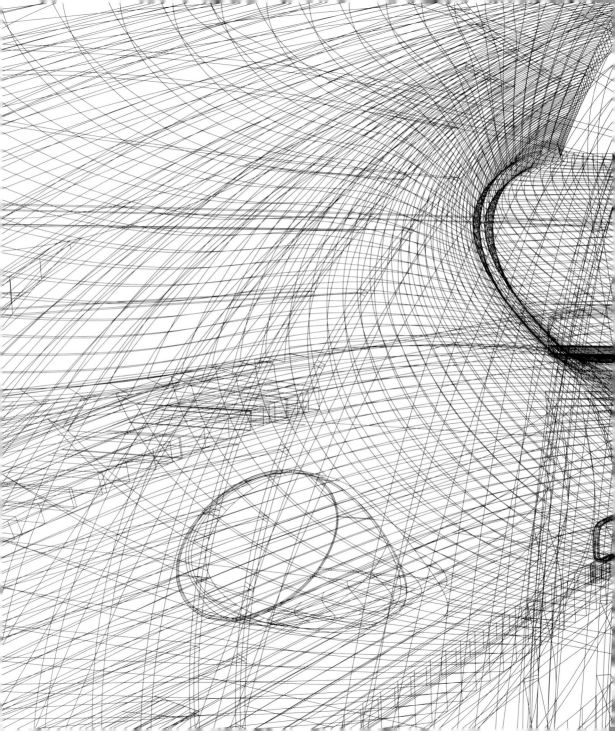

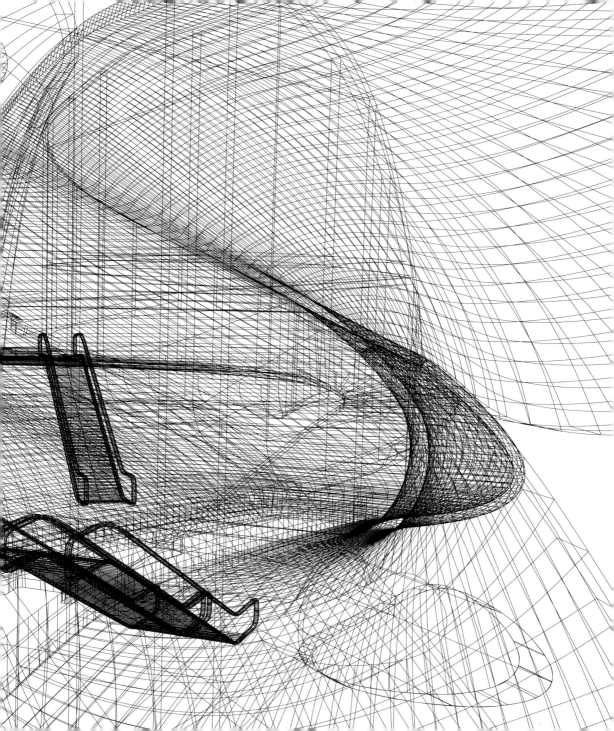

3
Scale-less-ness ... That Abstract Machine

Scale-less-ness is the capacity to operate at no scale, opening up multiple interpretations of meaning of the same configuration at different scales simultaneously. Scale-less-ness ... that abstract machine will address the question: how to invert data to be able to generate an operational methodology that can be implemented in the design process at different scales simultaneously? There is no doubt that scale is all about data and the scale is determined by the amount and kind of data that is embedded in the system. Therefore, we should start asking among other questions: what is data and why is it so important? Data collection from the recording of our observations is one of the primary steps to understanding the complexity and multiplicity of existing conditions. Data are numbers, characters, images, or other methods of recording, in a form that can be assessed by humans or (especially) input into computers, stored, and processed there, or transmitted digitally. Computers nearly always represent data in a binary format. Raw data is meaningless; only when interpreted by some kind of data processing system does it take on meaning and become information.

How are the processing and/or interpretation of data made possible? People or computers can find patterns in data to perceive information, and information can be used to enhance knowledge. Since knowledge is a prerequisite to wisdom, we always want more data and information. But, as modern societies verge on information overload, we especially need better ways to find patterns. Data in itself has no scale, only when filtered through diagrammatic techniques does it take on meaning and scale. The process of data becoming to scale is when the relationship architect-data is critical. It will determine and constrain the approach to project conceptualization and primary spatial relationships.

In the search for a method of diagramming new infrastructural trajectories—points of intersection and densifications within the networked urban landscape involving a non-existing necessity of scale suggesting—the visualization not of fragments, but of a whole, a shifting field that never differentiates points from lines, because one becomes the other and vice versa.

To encounter different qualities in the line, to synthesize flexible and dynamic networked fields of information in accordance with their scale-less capability, to behave as a shifting field; these have been brought to mutual potential by linking different programmatic networks in association with geometries and topological configurations, aligning to existing conditions, and visualizing their relationships at different scales simultaneously. The dynamic interchange of information between scales is correlated with orders of differences: level, temperature, pressure, tension, potential, intensity, etcetera. Intensity is the form of difference. Every intensity is differential, by itself a difference. How can we identify data patterns that operate as systems of differential intensities, and how can a system of differential intensities be implemented within the design process?

Patterns of differential intensities are generated by operations of striation and over-striation in order to understand qualities and properties embedded in the system of information depicted. Systematic operations of striation and over-striation are deployed in the existing cityscape to redefine its embedded information and to reconfigure a new system of information based on conditions of change. Affiliations by agglomeration of coded information emerge to be reinterpreted as systematic, continuous striation. Within each operative process, scale-less filtering of information is required to generate a qualified multilayered map which behaves as a shifting field, allowing multiple readings depending on the scale depicted and the parameters assigned.

Hence, the project Multi-Linear Fields was conceived. Responding to a brief seeking a new masterplan for the Docklands area of East London, the project first reconnects the surrounding roads currently severed at the outer boundaries of this undeveloped, post-industrial site. These structural lines are drawn across the site to set up a network of connections both internally, and in terms of the surrounding infrastructure. Alongside the digital design work, a series of physical models were made, less as representations of a proposed building strategy, and more as forms of material computation of the forces that determine the organizational diagrams of the site. Furthermore, the project addressed multilinear conditions such as trajectories and points of intersection, instrumentalized through diagrammatic techniques which allowed the scale-less development of the project. By intertwining multidirectional fields, static configurations were translated into interactive ones. Therefore, the project grasped issues of adaptability and temporality through various gradients of permanence, further implementing them to generate Management Organizations. Even before beginning the proposal, we had to collect a lot of information based on the project's requirements. We got a lot of data in the form of square meters. Therefore, it was important to create a process that allowed us to be operative and could answer the question: how do we treat data that is just defining the amount of square meters needed for a non-specific site? All the data collected striated the site, generating a striated space. We found those conditions in the project we did in Tono, Japan. What we proposed in Glowing Topologies: Toki Plasma Research Park, was to generate a smooth space by over-striating the data and the site. We deployed a dynamic glowing lighting system that striates the site, so we understand the site as a whole, and then, over-striates the lighting pattern, incorporating different lighting conditions that determine through interaction the degree of activity in the specific area. We filtered the data by inverting the process of generating scaled space. The data in square meters was transformed by the dynamic glowing lighting system into degrees of activity. Degrees of activities were understood as a dynamic system of intensities that will shape programmatic synergies into inhabitable space. Furthermore, variation-transformation-mutation processes were implemented as a stage of dynamic interaction between the architectural intervention and the existing environmental conditions. Indeed, those processes were based on the original data collected. The urban topology is transformed by the interaction of different parameters. Light is understood as a dynamic field of information, where simple expressions generate complex relationships of interaction. Transforming and deforming the consistent existing topological surface, light interaction generates and defines the surface appearance, dynamically changing its properties by reaction. Displacement and controlling parameters define the information flows, appearance, and materiality. Captured lighting patterns' movement within an endless system of operation is simplified to explore some possibilities of transfer phenomena, where the urban system is artificially manipulated and controlled by conscious operators.

Glowing Topologies was an experiment where fluctuating soft lighting patterns interact with each other and with the existing natural conditions to generate different programmatic environments. The result is an artificial-natural environment that fosters the breeding of new ideas and scientific breakthroughs in a scientific community, and provides a strong visual identity as part of Japan's new heart in the twenty-first century. We proposed a dynamic topological glowing system which will transform the urban topological surface by the interaction of different parameters. Therefore, light was understood as a dynamic field of information, where simple expressions generate complex

relationships of interaction. Transforming and deforming the consistent existing topological surface, light interaction generates and defines the surface appearance, dynamically changing its properties by reaction. Displacement and controlling parameters define the information flows, appearance, and materiality. Captured lighting patterns' movement within an endless system of operation is simplified to explore some possibilities of transfer phenomena, where the urban system is artificially manipulated and controlled by conscious operators. The skin is said to "glow" in response to program, existing conditions, and artificial conditions. A glowing volume appears curiously alive because of its dynamic variation by interaction. Artificial light signals the presence of activity, the energy that animates the environment. While fluctuating lighting systems serve to illuminate an object, environment, or task area, others emit low levels of light to emphasize the lighting fixture itself. Light emanates from soft, heavy blobs of gel or from bulbs festooned with silicone growths. While most lighting patterns must be shielded from touch, these objects invite physical contact. Their dull interior illumination draws attention to the surface, infusing their skins with an alien energy, at once comforting and strange. Lighting was conceived as a field of embedded information (expressions of information). Moreover, the glow is the addition of data within the space. People can read any area in terms of occupancy, type of area, type of work, and period of time. Embedded swamp areas, as well as water gardens, are included as a variation of the glow. As a result, we have glowing topologies which are dynamically fluctuating and generating different environmental configurations. In the process of expansion, the City-Scape abandoned growing as a whole, and deterritorialized voids emerged within the urban fabric—voids that consequently became marginalized and incapable of adapting and reconfiguring their urban activities. At the same time, condensation of functions and inhabitations in very reduced and specific locations were deterritorializing communities and public social activities. The urban fabric was reconfigured and reconsolidated by alienation of spaces. We can detect those urban conditions in the City-Scape which has been alienated by abandonment of site specifics. The City-Scape's urban voids reached a magnitude in scale to a degree that isolated communities which had been coexisting in the past. As a result, issues of race and social wealth were raised to determine the way in which different social groups re-territorialized the City-Scape. Hence, territorial boundaries were redefined from within, creating invisible boundaries—boundaries that no map will show to explain the City-Scape, but which are nevertheless real. These invisible boundaries are so real that we can see how they isolate communities and discriminate against social groups. Glowing Topologies' primary interest is to bond the City-Scape as a whole—understanding site-specific differences—making communities participate in the public social life. The second interest is to bring back the communities' identities, to involve people in public events, and community activities throughout the City-Scape. The proposal over-striates the urban fabric with a system of glowing topologies that acts as a global trigger for local actions throughout the City-Scape. Generating site-specific configurations according to each existing environment, Glowing Topologies will be an active element within each social community that triggers the reactivation of public activities and revitalizes public spaces to become the place where communities wish to be. In the search for a method of triggering communities' public activities, urban voids, and densifications that comprise the networked urban landscape, the City-Scape employs a non-existing necessity of scale—suggesting the visualization not of fragments, but of a whole, a shifting field that never differentiates points from lines because one becomes the other and vice versa. Sometimes, the conditions we had to consider were as open as they could be. For example, the following project had the site itself as one of the conditions. The proposal is deployed throughout the city and should be able to adapt to street level variations between 1 percent - 10 percent. With these and other conditions in mind, we developed our proposal, *Intelligent Surface: Media Platform for 2004 Olympic Games* (Athens, Greece).

The proposal re-interpreted City-Leisure Activities Generators appropriating the Greek cultural notion of public space, in particular the temple surroundings on the Acropolis, as a space of interaction; as well as the idea of journey, as an interior and virtual journey. We were interested in combining them to recover the idea of surprise in the event, as a surprise finding objects. The proposed topological configuration is simultaneously a place where visitors find an environmental space to plug in and log on, having access to any information they request; as well as a place to rest and start a "journey." Therefore, the proposal generated two environments connected by a metaphorical bridge: the exterior one is more a plug-in device display where visitors can feel that they arrived at a different place and can experience access to information; the interior one is lived as an open internal exteriority, because the visitor will be part of different gradients of filtered visuals. The visitor can participate from the exterior as a "voyeur," being part of a differently qualified space. The interior is expressing a different configuration from the exteriority, but in a virtual connection with the exteriority. The interior is clustered by a permeable, semi-translucent, flexible tubular membrane supported by laser-cut, stainless steel rings which host the tubular envelope. The tubular membrane embedded with glowing lighting patterns generate different environments, recreating the idea of staying in the interior of an organism. Artificial light and artificial life. The intelligent surface appears curiously alive because of its dynamic variation by interaction. Artificial light signals the presence of activity, the energy that animates the environment. While lighting patterns illuminate an envelope, a new environment is developed, inviting physical contact in its interior illumination and infusing the skins with an alien energy, at once comforting and strange. The structure itself represents the evolution of a "primitive topology." The transformation is the genesis of space and opens up a new kind of permeability and connectivity with the exteriority. The project aims to realize mutations and transformations of space through spatial changes and transitions of surface. To mutate and to transform physical space, different glowing techniques were implied to create a more dynamic structural system. Significantly, the structural system is not aggressive with the existing conditions; the object places itself in a soft manner. The structure poses itself without being attached to the ground. The structure is protecting itself from exterior aggressions with stainless steel rings that expose to the exterior when they get close to the ground. Otherwise, the ring is always in the interior. The surface exposes its softness and a variety of effects—especially when the volume reaches a non-human high. The structural system is a combination of a rigid system and a flexible system which is composed of perforated, laser-cut, stainless steel rings hosting semi-translucent PVC tubes (flexible structural system). The structure is easily mounted by locating the bottom part of the stainless steel rings and the horizontal pre-curved stainless steel tube. After the rings are in place and attached to the c-shape stainless steel internal ring, the structure is ready to receive the upper stainless steel rings which are screwed to the bottom rings. After tightening them with the upper interior ring, we place the tubes by sliding them through the structure perforations. At the same time, the electrical glowing lighting system has to be placed. Finally, and after the interior platform is located, the equipment can be displayed. The required volume to store the structure and transportation is around 16.2 cubic meters. We recommend dividing the volume as follows: PVC tubular structure (8 cubic meters); stainless steel rings (128 cubic meters); container 8 x 8 x 2 meters); media station unit and lighting (4 cubic meters). The rough cost estimate is around USD 200,000, based on USD 100,000 for the structure, USD 25,000 for the lighting, and USD 20,000 per Media Station Unit. In other cases, we worked with the space of mediation between the intervention and the environmental conditions. The outcome was a volumetric skin, not a membrane nor a surface, but a volume specifically embedded with coded information that defines its generation process. The coded information is the equilibrium between the proposed conditions and the given conditions. The coded information defines changes in skin thickness, variation in materiality, as well as volumetric displacements. That means that coded information defines space. Therefore, coded information is to scale. Through observation, we noticed that there were several fields of forces that torqued, twisted, and mutated the volume of air in the site. It was very interesting to understand how different environmental conditions defined a quantum flow that configured particular conditions in the site. Therefore, we decided that the first approach should focus on the interaction between the data given in square meters and the environmental conditions detected in the site. At this moment, we started to script the volume with embedded information that would allow us to change and transform those predetermined conditions and generate new conditions. Through the process, some primary conditions were preserved as some others changed. Thus, the museum is experienced in a twisted, 3D looped circuit through distinctly shaped spaces.

The lighting concept is defined by two different lighting behaviors that relate to each other based on their differences. Outdoor lighting embedded on the skin reacts to existing environmental conditions. Indoor lighting creates internal environmental conditions. Outer skin collects energy during the daytime and glows at night. Condensing natural light and glowing artificially makes the proposal seemingly alive, and it becomes an iconic image of the city. The internal lighting environment creates a new universe; differentiating from the exteriority, creating an artificial/natural lighting interior landscape. We explored the relationship between artificial light and artificial life. Therefore, the thickened skin is meant to "glow" in response to program, existing conditions, and proposed artificial conditions. As a result, the glowing volume appears curiously alive because of its dynamic variation by interaction. Artificial light signals the presence of activity from the energy that animates the environment. While fluctuating lighting systems serve to illuminate the proposal, the environment, or task areas, emit low levels of light to foreground the light-ing fixture itself. The light emanates from soft, heavy volumes of gel or from bulbs festooned with silicone growths. While most lighting patterns must be shielded from touch, these objects invite physical contact. The soft interior illumination draws attention to the surface, infusing the skin with an alien energy, at once comforting and strange. The proposed glowing volume hosts differentiated glowing volumes which are dynamically fluctuating, generating different environmental configurations. This is the case with the project in Suwon, South Korea: *Museum in TL-SYNC*, Nam June Paik Museum. The museum is a dynamic environmental system that is constantly shifting to achieve its system ideal process.

The project name is composed of two acronyms:

SYNC

1. To synchronize, to bring into synchronization.
2. <file system> to force ("flush") all pending buffered disk writes to the disk.
3. More generally, to force a number of competing processes or agents to a state that would be "safe" if the system were to "crash," i.e., to checkpoint in the database sense.

TL

1. Twisted loop. System ideal process key-component that stabilizes and constantly shifts into flex_net (flexible networks) dynamic configurations.

We took as our starting point the image of Nam June Paik with *Demagnetizer* (*Life Ring*), 1965. We analyzed it and understood *Demagnetizer* as an intervention in the field of forces that transforms the existing field of conditions, generating new configurations in the field. We worked conceptually to address those aspects with *TL-SYNC*. The existing field of conditions was the topography, and by interweaving the topography patterns it became a topological entity. The transformation was defined by a generation of new patterned configurations. As the topography is represented by 2D lines, the topology is represented by 3D lines that "navigate" in space, generating a new patterned network. Another work from Paik that we used as reference was *TV Crown* (1999 version). Paik manipulated television with signal amplifiers; color, silent.

Sequence_1 and Sequence_2 show a 3D loop expansion-compression and the interaction between positive and negative space. Both of the sequences have as the main structure a 3D loop. *TV Buddha* (1974) addressed the notion of infinite temporal loop. The 3D loop is defined by the relationship of humanized objects. Therefore, the proposal for *Museum in TL-SYNC* incorporates the notion of infinite temporal 3D loop. The 3D twisted loop compresses and expands according to the program and becomes the "navigational" link to the qualified spaces.

The lobby is the main entry situated at an important distance from the street, approached in a gradual, diagonally elevated transition. A visual connection between the lobby and the site-specific installations, and direct access to all parts of the exhibition make the lobby the center point of the twisted loop. The entry area has escalators to provide access from the street level, and a direct shortcut connection to the changing exhibitions. Nam June Paik's installation is enclosed by a U-shaped double wall that contains a ramp to the upper exhibition level. With different degrees of transparency, the wall is a crucial element of the space and its interaction with the artist's work. It acts as a double-sided projection screen and backdrop for elements of the installation. The ramp and the visitors using it become part of the space, as their blurred movement blends

with the projected images. The floor is tilted, providing a height between six and ten meters. The museum's exhibition and circulation concept is experienced in a twisted, looped 3D circuit through distinctly shaped spaces. The exhibition is organized through a continuous sequence starting with the installation, going up to the special project gallery, the permanent exhibition, and down again to the changing exhibition. A variation of the circuit includes the sculpture garden. Frequent visitors may have direct access to the changing exhibition. All curatorial, administration, and service functions are contained in a hovering sculptural volume, leaving the exhibition spaces open and fluid, and providing the visitor with a continuous spatial experience. As the heart of the museum, the Nam June Paik Gallery is located on the upper exhibition level. The varying ceiling height between four and ten meters and a transition from natural to artificial light accommodate the entire range of Nam June Paik's objects and installations. The special project gallery is situated at the south end of the space, on top of the installation. It can be programmatically connected both to the permanent and the changing exhibition, accommodating exhibitions of different sizes with its height of nine meters. The permanent exhibition continues on a wide ramp downward and blends into the changing exhibition. Nam June Paik's work will be confronted and interact with the work of contemporary South Korean and international artists. The replica of the artist's studio is an integral part of the permanent exhibition at the north end of the upper level. The changing exhibition is situated on a continuous slope and leads the visitor back to the lobby. After completion of the final phase, the Nam June Paik Museum complex will serve as an internationally known center for video and media arts. Our goal was to create a vivid environment for both the reception and production of avant-garde art. Therefore, the focus was on a close spatial and programmatic relationship between the museum and the Media Art Research & Education Center (MARC) in order to stimulate exchange on all levels and the breeding of new ideas and concepts. The two buildings will be distinct but closely linked. The main entrance of the research center will be on street level below the museum lobby. Another entrance will be on the lobby level. Artists will have direct access to the facilities and resources of the museum, and vice versa. MARC houses a dormitory in the same building in order to foster the artists' community and create a lively working environment. In this context, the main auditorium is considered a crucial element and focus point for the museum to stimulate discourse between artists, researchers, and the general public, and will be included in the initial phase, along with the first extension of the exhibition space. The further extension of exhibition and storage space will connect the museum with MARC. A linear extension of the underground parking towards the south is possible as required. A different situation arose when we were asked to design an art gallery in New York.

Onishi Gallery / Gallery Memoria, located in Chelsea, the heart of Manhattan's contemporary art scene, was conceived as a mediating space. The space was designed to enhance the moment for contemplation—differentiated for the contemplation of art and traditionally crafted altars from Japan. The gallery space has a special relationship with the street level. Therefore, it was critical to establish a strong connection with the street level by designing a continuous spatial transition without blocking the gallery's view from the street. The continuous spatial transition occurs in the vertical and horizontal plane, by folding continuous surfaces that guide our perception while navigating the differentiated gallery space. The differentiation of space is determined by moments of transition between the different surfaces, exposing the perceptual continuity of the gallery. This spatial continuity is articulated by the reception desk which becomes the hinge between two programmatically distinct spaces. Tectonics' color was a determinant component in our design, as white was the unique color on our palette. Indeed, we took that constraint as a challenge and worked within the material's surfaces, developing a white sensitive skin. Therefore, we incorporated the lighting as an interface between the skin of the surface and the visitor. Furthermore, the white epoxy floor was the most important horizontal element which contributed to unifying the space and bonding the two differentiated spaces into one. The intention of the polished white epoxy floors was to make the walls seem to levitate, and thereby enhance the contemplation experience. The visitor will feel like he or she is floating on an ethereal surface. Despite the physical condition of our bodies, the space was designed to liberate our physical condition when entering the gallery space. The photos by Seong Kwon present the project with a strong contrast of light and color between the interior and exterior, depicting the intended differentiation between interiority and exteriority. Indeed, while we were inside the gallery space, it was very important to capture the sensitive ethereal variations of white perceptions within the gallery space surfaces. Scale-less-ness is a property embedded as much in these projects as in the abstract machine that urges for an active positioning towards adaptable environments by capturing dynamic interactions between the architectural intervention and the environment.

Onishi Gallery / Gallery Memoria, New York

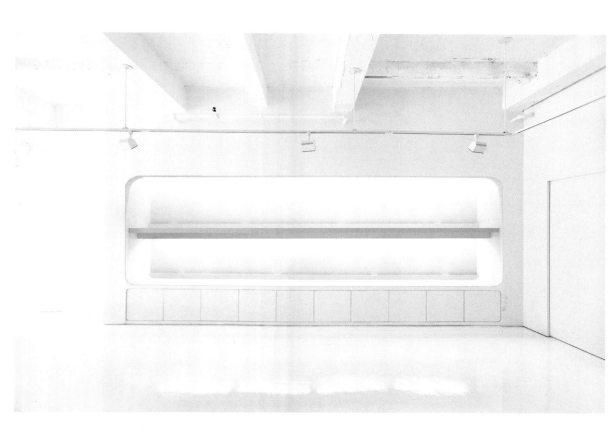

Disembodiment. Berlin

JOSÉ SALINAS/
KNOBSDesign
Disembodiment

8.3. - 3.5.08

n intimac(it)y

A trans Pavilion curated by Isolde Nagel

Hackesche Höfe Hof III. Rosenthalerstr. 40/41 10178 Berlin

www.atransberg +49 (0)173.2025920

Sponsored by

Botschaft von Spanien, Berlin
Ministerio de Cultura, Madrid
Foto Lautenschlager AG, St. Gallen
ILFOCHROM Faulin
Siegler & Dürr Stiftung
Stiftung Stadtkreditbank GmbH Stiftung
Akademie der Künste, Berlin

4
Shiftments: A Perspective on Nomadic Monads

What does it mean to think, and to reorient oneself in a system that has lost the conventions of its Euclidian skin? Seeking a position in a system that is constantly changing and reshaping itself according to exterior forces, new "shiftment" strategies are developed, generating a simultaneous shifting from an absolute positioning to a relative positioning. Therefore, new systems of representation were developed, allowing us to forfeit a deeper understanding of our dynamic positioning within architecture. An example of those new systems of representation is the line. The line, understood as a diagrammatic technique, is a vector; a direction and not a dimension or metric determination. It is a relationship constructed by local operations involving changes of direction. The line is filled by events and is a space of effects, more than properties. It is a logic of unfinished series, system of coordinates and dynamic orientations. As objects turn to codes, colors, and intensities, processes of coding and decoding information restructure themselves to develop new systems of information. The system depicts its own territory, while movements of deterritorialization and process-

es of reterritorialization are developed. When these processes take place, the diagram reconfigures itself from the centroide to its periphery and then from the new centroide to the new periphery. The system is organized by a greater deterritorialization, as the process advances and keeps moving further away from its initial configuration. The system and the associations of one particular set of information with another move through different strata towards spaces of alternative, which are the states of the in-between, some stable, others volatile. Its existence is transitory and ephemeral, behaving as incorporations to one or another. Their relations are not quite localized, as the system is characterized by speeds within the strata. It is possible to establish horizontal levels as the diagram is read in a vertical way, or vertical if the reading is done in a horizontal way, executing an elementary Cartesian reading of the diagram. This reading of the diagram is absolutely literal and fails to represent what the diagram depicts. What happens with the different levels of understanding in the many possible directions is what states the diagram's possibilities of development. This type of diagram gives the possibility for multiplicity in order to achieve different ranges of associations, allowing the existence of spaces of alternatives and nomadic flows. Nomadic flows would generate movements of reterritorialization, as they move independently through different strata's systems of reference. It is possible to say that more important than the information mapped originally in the diagram are the new configurations rendered in the diagram as it develops, and its capacity to do so when it is torn into its components. In this type of diagram, the diagonals operate in an unmeasured form in its own centroide, moving towards the periphery, colonizing it, and reconfiguring a new periphery, opening the possibility for new information to be captured. In this way, movements are generated on an indefinite basis by the information; establishing micro-systems inside the diagram where the information crashes, finding new paths, et cetera. As the information stabilizes itself in the strata, it is possible to say that it becomes sedimentary, at least in a short-term span. These would be called short-term information alternative zones. These nodes of concentration of information belong to a process in which speed is entirely different to the later processes generated. This phenomenon is to be observed as something extremely positive, because when these consequences become non-tolerable, the life span of the short-term information alternative zones comes to its end, and becomes the catalyst for a reorganization of these zones into other alternative zones that are, in fact, more suited to the existing conditions. The diagram renders alternatives behaving as a nomadic monad. Nevertheless, the diagram is not an animation or a simulation that literally represents alternatives of association or exchange of information. The diagram expresses a nomadic monad, because it does

not limit itself to a particular set of possibilities within an isolated system; rather, it opens up an infinite range of possibilities, thus qualifying as a dynamic system. Its dynamism is not present in the sense that it has redundant motion, but in the sense of what happens in the system is dependent on speeds. The dynamic diagram has certain qualities within itself that urge constant rereading and redefinition in order to become the proper tool to understand the nomadic monads. The diagram renders alternatives as it behaves as a nomadic monad.

5
Topological Body vs. Euclidean Body

Leonardo da Vinci's *Vitruvian Man* (1513) encloses an ideal (generic) human body within a square and a circle, establishing it as the origin of all systems of proportion. Indeed, Renaissance anthropocentric society hinged on this link between man and space. At the time, the square and the circle represented the basis of geometrical form, and thus of all systems of depiction. The body, then, was the measure not only of science (geometry, physics) but of decoration as well (geometrical depiction). What about the twenty-first century body? Is the notion of a generic ideal still valid? Can it hold the same privileged place as it did in the Renaissance? Are the square and the circle still sufficient to establish a link—the body to proportion—or do we need to look elsewhere? The *Vitruvian Man* was drawn, following tradition, in frontal view. Therefore, if we consider the square as a cube or a cylinder, and the circle as a sphere, we can begin to readdress the conditions of the *Vitruvian Man*. Indeed, we may consider each volume as a set of properties or environmental conditions which locate the body within a broader context. The body itself, does not comprise a proportional system, but rather is comprised by the interaction of multiple systems. Furthermore, it depicts the body in a multidimensional space. This is a crucial development, and establishes a new paradigm for understanding the body's relationship to depiction. The body has historically been a resource, a canon to establish systems of proportion external to the systems of the body itself. Geometry is an over-simplification instrument. It defines the relationship between a whole and its parts. Measuring the body through an external metric system such as geometry can only yield known quantities and static relationships, while considering the body through a system of information embedded within, such as topology, reveals and describes a whole greater than the sum of its parts.

The belly is the body's origin; regardless of whether it is understood as a geometrical system or a topological system. The belly, the mysterious place where life takes shape, is the point of continuity between exterior and interior, between a surface and its depth and extensions. In recent years, a deeper understanding of these relationships has been possible through instrumental tools and applications specifically developed to look at the body in a different way; a new perspective that can interpret the complexity of the systems of information embedded within, and bring them to surface.

"José Salinas investigates the creation of synthetic architectural bodies that are reactive to external forces. His first approach in the project Topological Diagrams is to start with a simple 3D volumetric form or geometric primitive and apply external forces in order to have the form mutate and develop its constantly changing and unique topology. His second approach is in the Hermeneutic Topologies sequence that shows the formation of a synthetic body through the process of applying external fields of forces to a flat surface. In the evolution of the flat surface to the skin and volume of the form, the attribution of the character of the synthetic body occurs. Salinas believes that this body is developed through an asexual processing of information and that the body is constructed through machinist operations. The form is not gendered in its evolution, nor is it after its completion. It is an interesting point that could be further developed as it pertains to the evolution and eventual deterioration of bodies and form. These projects point to a departure from the metaphors of smoothness and organic shapes as merely representations of the biological to a development of architecture through processes that are fundamentally more biological. Architects work with raw computational power to evolve 'self-generating' architectural scenarios. This has led to a move away from the interest in smooth surfaces with an emphasis on the interaction of individual cellular elements. It is essential to note, however, that the smooth and the discrete are merely understood at the level of scale. This is especially the case in architecture. In a smooth model of

skin, at the level of the glossy rendered image, the architecture is luminous, luscious, reflective, and absolutely seamless—just like bodies. But architecture is made of smaller discrete units that must come together to make surfaces. We can think of the skin as a parametric system that is continuous in the change from one area to another but also discrete because it is made up of individual cells or elements. If we are to map the surface or skin (of a body) in detail, then we must engage the discrete and cellular phenomena that produce it. At the same time, if we are to appreciate what these phenomena produce, then we must reengage the topological identities that emerge from them. What are the ways by which architecture can engage this co-presence of the smooth and the discrete?"[2]

Looking at the body to explore architectural possibilities is something that was explored during the Renaissance. Hence, we started working, focusing on the head and developing the work *Hermeneutic Topologies*, finding the soil to explore issues of machinistic identities and appearance. *Hermeneutic Topologies* is a computer animation in three parts: "scanning, processing, and retrieving." Played in a sequence, these animations loop endlessly on a large projection wall, or a video monitor. It investigates a fictive, recognition-decryption process, suggesting that an image scan generates a 3D visualization of your virtually generated appearance. Upon "scanning," a topological scan of the tonal properties of the image is created by the rendering of a software recognition framework—in this case lighting recognition system—hence augmenting the information to alter or mutate. "Processing," the second stage, implements a new set of parameters to interpret the collected information into yet another tonal scale pattern. The third part is the "retrieval." Based on the data processed in sec-

2 Alicia Imperiale "Seminal Space: Getting Under the Digital Skin." Re: Skin. MIT Press 2007

tions one and two, it unfolds the information via dynamic processing that finds its volumetric virtual appearance, readdressing the original photograph of the person scanned. The next step is to continue working on the head and add the torso as another part of a generic body. Thus, *Genomic Herm_A(phrodite)* was produced. *Genomic Herm_A(phrodite)*, is a sociological portrait map depicted on the body. It emerged from an exploration of Synthetic Generic Bodies generated by machinist environmental systems. This exploration reflects psychological implications of the relationship between the body and the machinist environment. This raises the question: will machines take into consideration issues of gender while generating the generic body? Will the generic body be the sum of both male and female, or neither? *Genomic Herm_A(phrodite)* addresses these questions with a body in constant change, reflected in the consolidation of dynamic information processing within its skin. The body is made generic through the depiction of patterned information across its surface features, within an environment fully controlled by systematized machined processes that constrain and condition our interactions. *Genomic Herm_A(phrodite)* is ultimately the struggle of a synthetic generic body within a pre-determined environment. Once *Genomic Herm_A(phrodite)* was completed, we felt we had developed a consistent methodology to approach the complexity of a full body. Therefore, we continued to work on systemizing our method and the responsiveness of our operations' sensitivity to a topological, generic full body. Thus, we started the ambitious project *Asymmetrical Body: Spirit Away* which explored the condition of the body under external conditions. The body is always processing and assimilating moments of maximum topological fluctuation,

forcing it to perform in moments of maximum equilibrium. The topological body is continuously under fluctuating stress, decomposing and reconfiguring its geometrical condition. *Asymmetrical Body: Spirit Away* depicts this struggle to reconfigure and adapt the internal conditions of the body to its surrounding conditions by a thickening of the topological skin with layers of information and pattern. In 2005, KNOBSDesign was invited by the prestigious AedesEast Gallery to exhibit our current work. The exhibition was very successful, and gave us confidence to continue our work. In 2008, we were invited to do an installation at A trans Pavilion in Berlin. After completing the installation, we felt that our work had reached a higher level of consistency, and it was a moment of materialization of all spatial investigations and formal explorations since starting the development of *Hermeneutic Topologies* in 2002. The solo installation project received international reviews: "With *Disembodiment*, José Salinas explores the obscure relationship between the body and its urban context. The visitors to the A trans Pavilion in Berlin, who came to see the José Salinas *Disembodiment* installation, were definitely in for an unusual art experience. Cubes (made of GFRP waffle mold material) were lined up in rows, forcing the visitor to jump from one island to the next, turning the show into a rather cumbersome balancing act. Attendees were able to experience first-hand the mission behind Salinas's work, namely to shed light on the obscure and intimate relationship between architecture, the body and the individual's interiority. The Spanish architect's spatial artwork proves that an architectural setting and environment may subconsciously influence our mind and consequently our body. In this 'simulation', the visitor goes through a process of disembodiment which mirrors an experience that we all may have in our own daily urban contexts. 'Disembodiment is a process of becoming.' Meaning: inner areas penetrate into outer areas; the individual's interiority becomes one with their surroundings. The same way our skin is sensitive to light and climate, our subconscious is sensitive towards shapes and surfaces. Modeled after Greek and Egyptian sculpture, representations of female and male heads in black, white, and green depicted on high definition Ilfochromes are the centerpiece of the installation. The images, which are positioned in a grid, reflect the structure of buildings and, moreover, combine the organic and the constructed. Architecture and body melt into one. Salinas's Disembodiment blends art, design, and architecture into a unique configuration that merges the installation perfectly into its city surroundings with the help of the showroom's large windows. Disembodiment, a solo installation in 2008 at A trans Pavilion at Hackesche Höfe Berlin, curated by Isolde Nagel, within the framework of the exhibition series 'An intimac(it)y'."[3]

The A trans Pavilion is located in a very particular urban condition. Its interior is directly exposed to the surrounding urban context, with which it manifests a strong connection. The installation explored the strength of this connection by generating an interior living space which exposed the individual's personal and disembodied interiority to the embodied or disembodied context. The interior was experienced as an intimate lived space set on an elevated artificial level, one surrounded by high definition Ilfochromes presenting the relationship Body–Building–City within its skin. The installation photos by Hiepler, Brunier captured the intimate relationship between the artificiality of the interior spaces we inhabit and the artificial urban context that surrounds our living spaces. The interior space projects onto the exterior becoming part of the urban context and the exterior urban context is perceptually integrated in the interiority of the gallery space. Indeed, the photos capture the perception and sense of space changing through time, as lighting conditions change the reflections and color interactions between the urban context and the gallery space, thereby reinforcing the interactions between our intimacy, living space, and urban context.

3 Ciba XYMARA project review:http://www.xymara.com/inmyx/index/inmyx608/act-200806-index/act-200806-josesalinas.htm

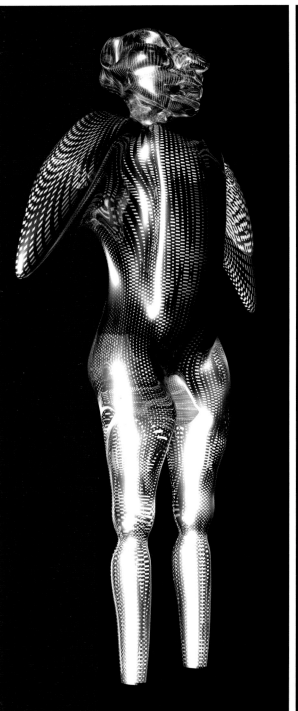

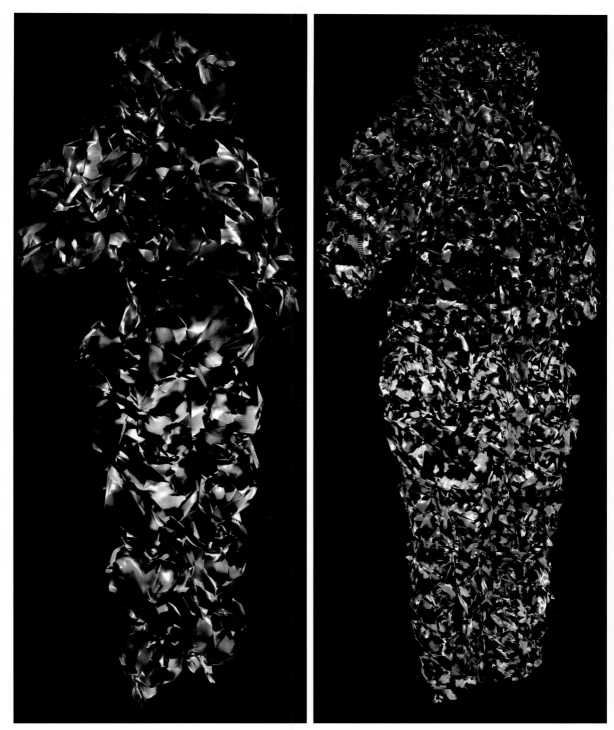

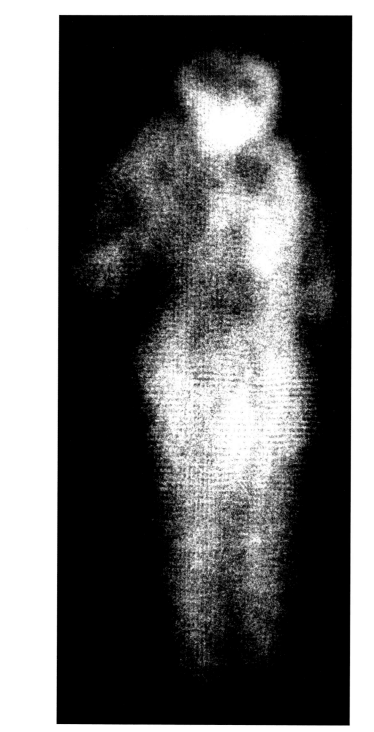

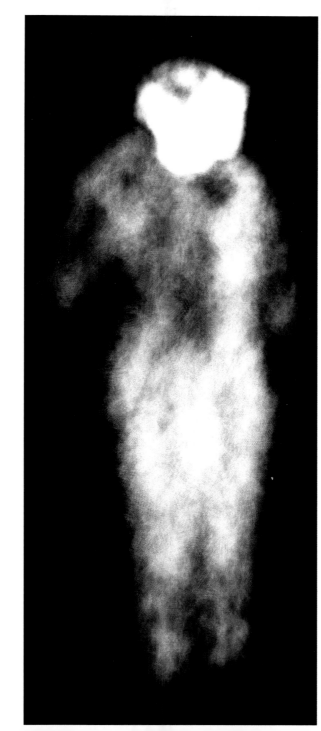

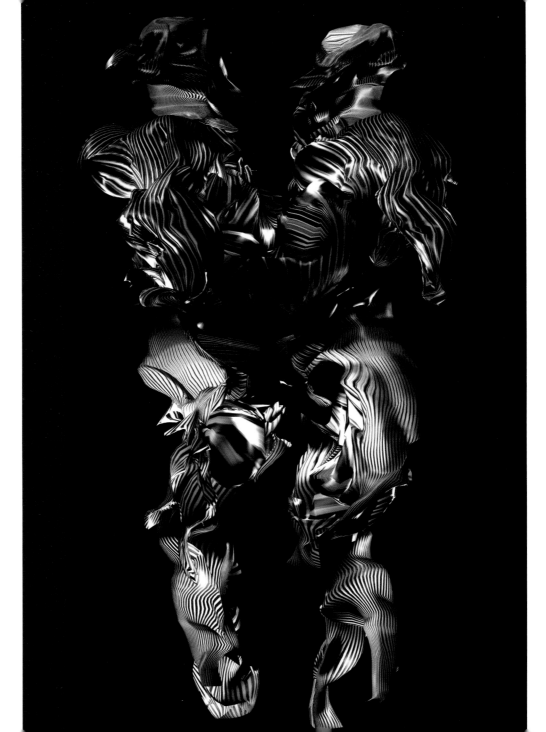

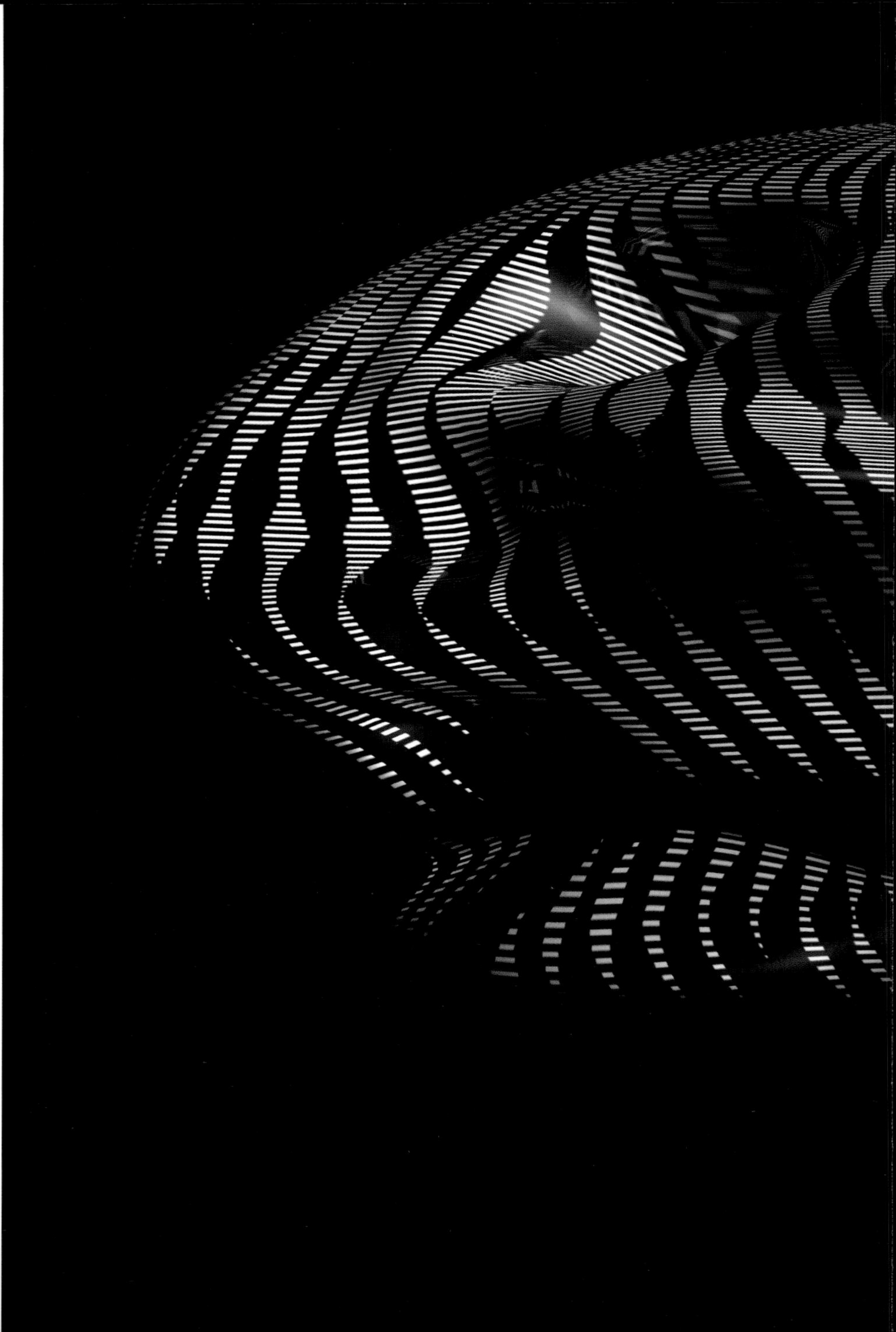

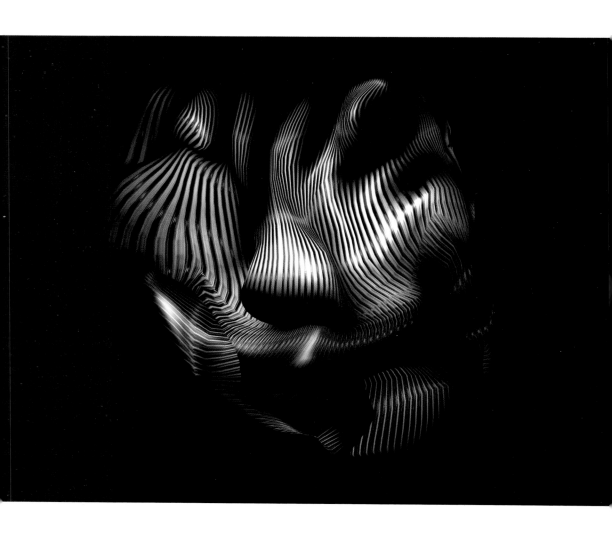

Topological Body vs. Euclidean Body

Topological Body vs. Euclidean Body

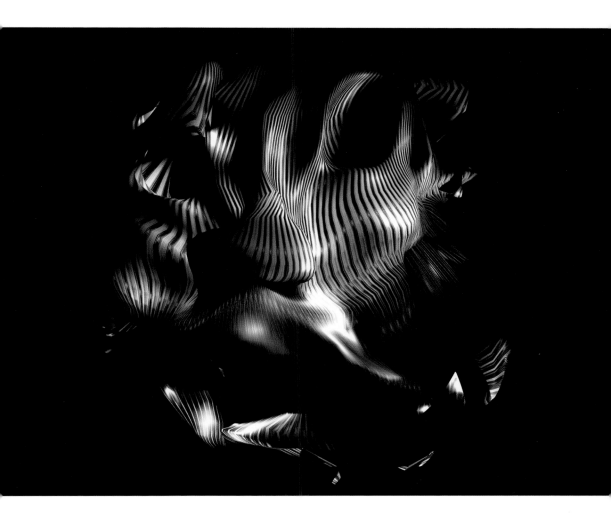

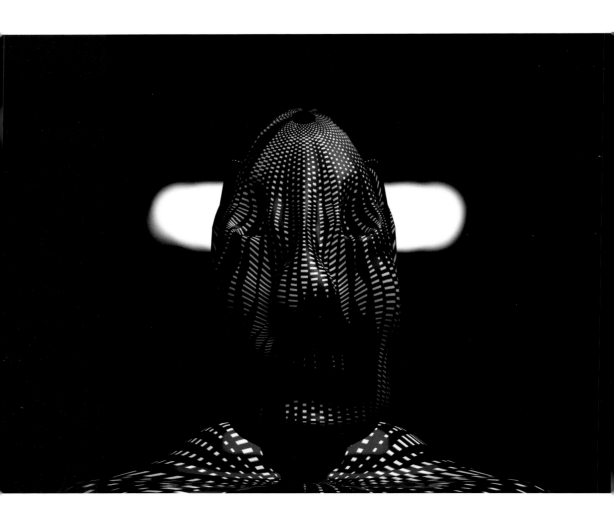

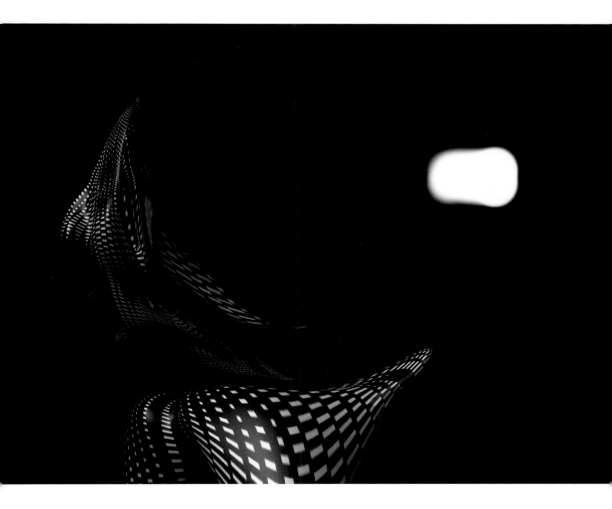

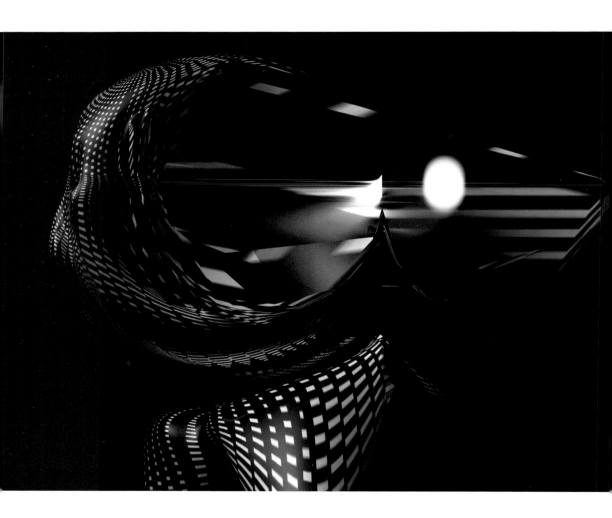

Topological Body vs. Euclidean Body

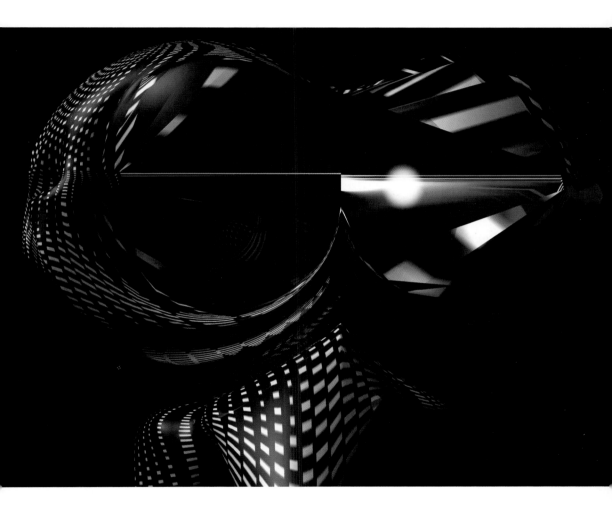

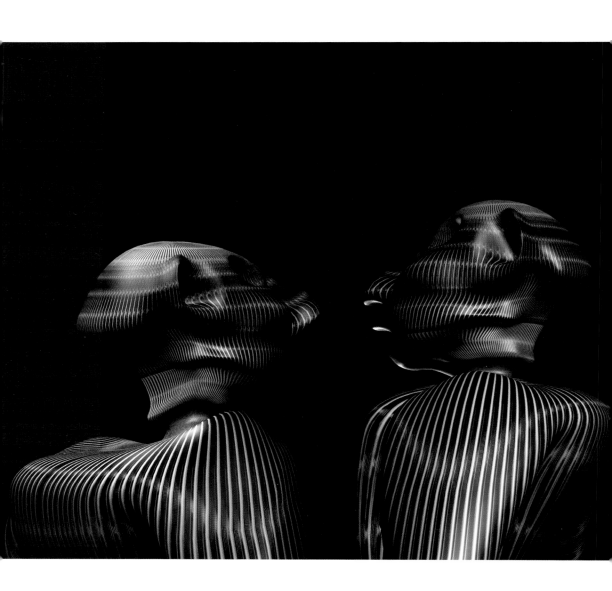

Topological Body vs. Euclidean Body

Topological Body vs. Euclidean Body

Topological Body vs. Euclidean Body

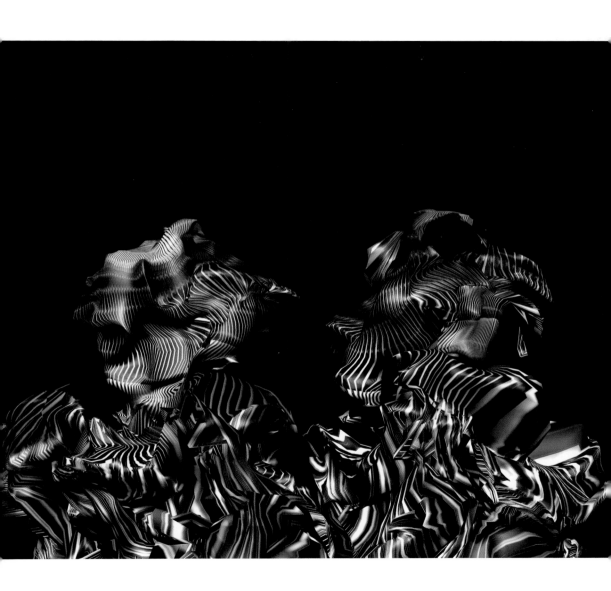

6
Toroidal_Scapes

Toroidal Landscapes is an ongoing project that explores continuity as a potential for developing a design method that goes beyond form and matter. With that objective, we chose a topology that was continuous in both directions [u,v], the torus; and configured continuous sets of transformations that will be applied to the torus using computational animated techniques. Therefore, time was another continuum parameter incorporated in the process.

With the intention of applying a consistent systematic set of transformations to the specific topology—in order to understand its behavior under the same changing set of conditions—we started with a single torus [A], and then with two tori, one of them rotated (0,90,0) from the torus geometric center of the other [B]. As all transformations were applied using computational animation techniques, all transformations must be seen in sequence. Indeed, the same sets of transformations were applied to [A] and [B], with clearly differentiated outcomes. After the first transformation, the directions [u,v] remained continuous. Therefore, we realized that the differentiated systematic transformations should enhance the topological continuity and

bring it to its limits. It was interesting to understand the internal logic of the torus behavior under the same set of conditions that will affect them. We evaluated some outcomes and established the logic of the possible variations. Moreover, as the process was implied and continued developing, we started to identify certain properties in the animated form and its visualization which we linked with architectural formations and materializations of continuous circulation systems.

Although we are working within the scale-less-ness capability of the method, we did define the topological organizational pattern which brought light to the potential material organizational pattern. Therefore, the way we first modeled the torus was very important, and had very important consequences. In fact, we developed these modeling techniques in the project for Athens, where the topological pattern and the material pattern were taken into consideration from the beginning and were carried all along the process until the final stage of the project. Consistently, five sets of transformations were applied continuously, one after the other. In other words, we applied the first set of transformations, evaluated the first outcome; subsequently we applied the second transformation to the first outcome, evaluated the second outcome; and then, applied the third transformation to the second outcome, evaluated the third outcome. We continued to implement the set of transformation until we had evaluated the fifth outcome. This is the current stage, and we are presenting this project in this book as an open-ended path of exploration, and it will be up to us to determine where it leads.

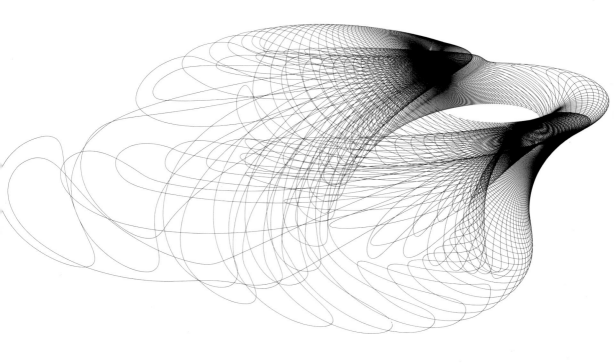

Topological Body. Parametric Sections

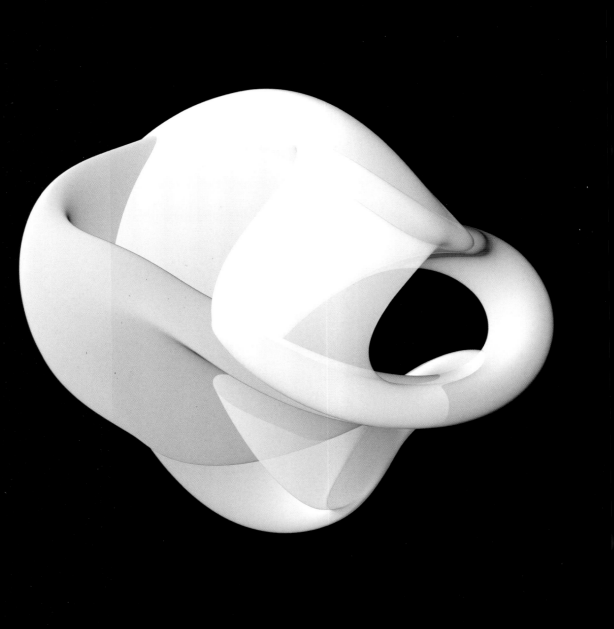

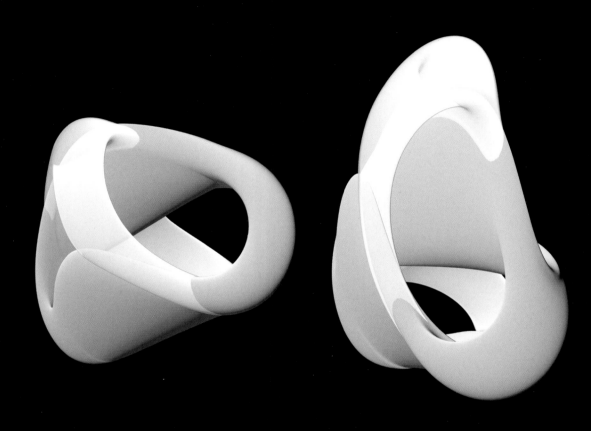

Toroidal Landscapes. Madrid

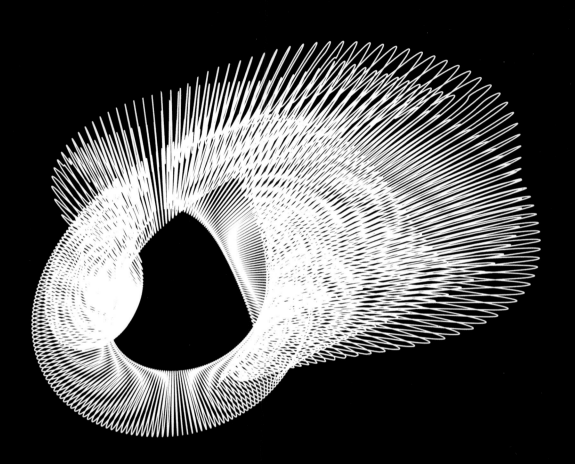

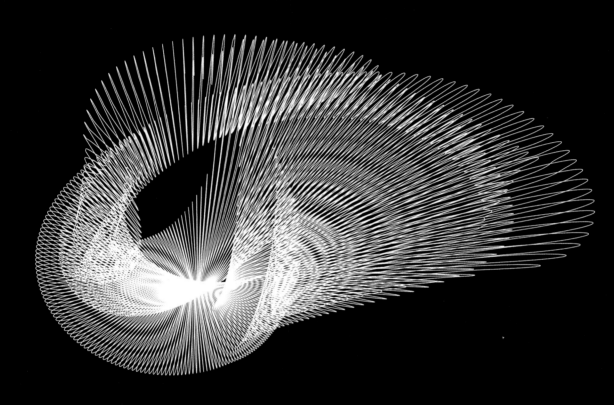

7
Disembodiment, a Process of Becoming

Disembodiment:
1. To free (the soul or spirit) from the body.
2. To divest of substance.

Disembodiment is a process of becoming, a consequence of the body occupying and experiencing the city, and one that divests our bodies of their material existences, distorting and transforming our physical states by increasing the a priori un-sensed condition to a point where we are able to perceive more clearly the distance between and/or the border separating our bodies and our minds. The various environments and living spaces accommodated by the city provoke differing processes of disembodiment, and these generate processes of alienation within the body, and also, in human identity and behavior. The intimate relationship between the city and the body is critical to determining our personal interpretation of the existing. The city is an environment made up of space and energy, one composed of undetected forces and synergies that are bound together by multiplicity and complexity. Indeed, the body is also an environment, it is also space and energy, and it is also composed of undetected forces and synergies that bring together the multiplicity and complexity of its topological configurations. It is the aim of the present conclusion to claim the importance of the intertwining extensions of our body and mind—within themselves and the exteriority—for developing a generative process. We are always seeking to generate an intimate relationship between the site and the proposal. For that matter, it is necessary to allow movements of deterritorialization between our body and mind. These movements have been previously explored. I recall Salvador Dali's *Paranoic Critic Method* and Jean Dubuffet's *Mescaline Landscapes* series. Moreover, we should explore our "intimate" relationships with the exteriority, in order to project ourselves to the exteriority and develop a generative design process which could become a design methodology.

During several conversations in different cafes in New York, Berlin, Madrid, and especially after completion of the solo installation *Disembodiment* at A trans Pavilion in Berlin and in the Weissenhof Architecture Gallery in Stuttgart in 2008, we realized that it was a very important moment for KNOBSDesign to revisit the work and unfold concepts developed during all these years. We used this time to make an important effort to systemize the consistency of our working processes and methodologies, of our theories (which sometimes had been imprecise), and our built projects and site-specific installations. The questions we have posed concerning design processes and methodologies have been purposely condensed, but these questions—when developed consistently—pass beyond the boundaries of architecture. As a discipline, architecture has always been supported by the working processes developed through the years, and by looking at other disciplines and incorporating the "filtered" ideas from those disciplines into our own design processes. Indeed, with the availability of new tools, techniques, and media, it has been critical to develop an adaptable conceptual consistency within the design process.

In this book, we expressed an important emphasis on the preciseness of visualizing one's thoughts, retrieving them in a maleable format that can be operative and allowing one to develop them consistently; it becomes a generative process.

Therefore, the aim of this book was to present KNOBSDesign, founded in New York in 2002, and our continuously evolving positioning towards architecture.

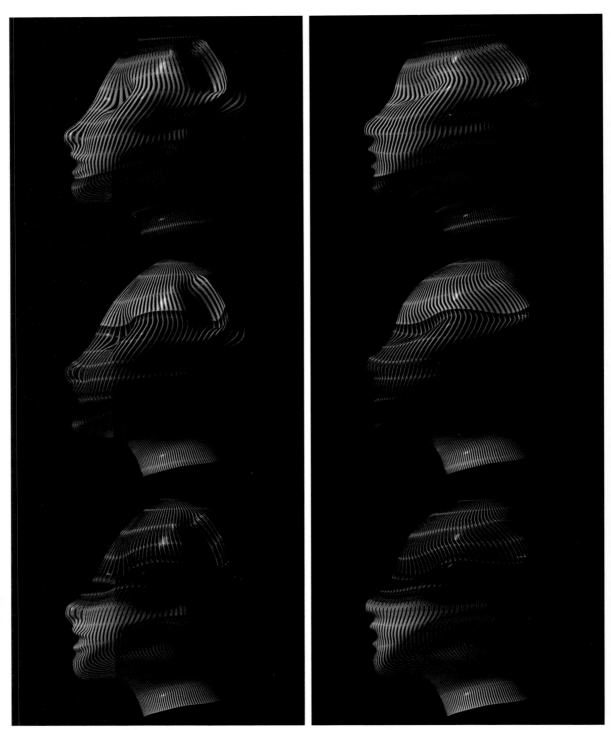

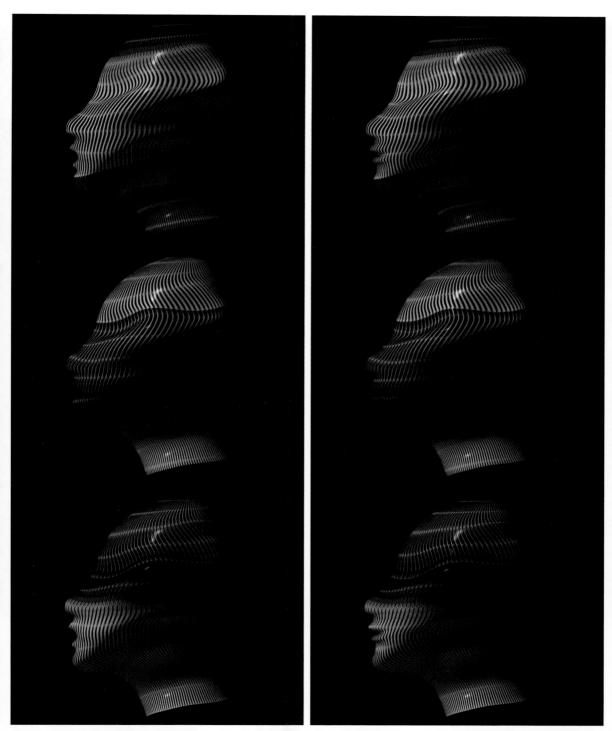

Disembodiment, a Process of Becoming

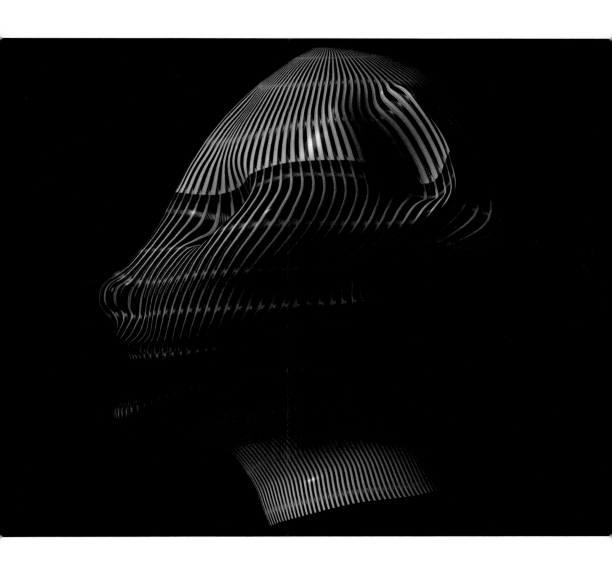

Disembodiment, a Process of Becoming

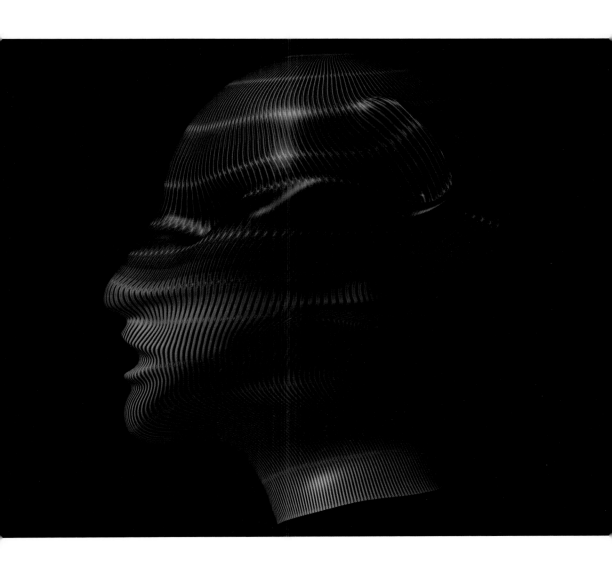

Freeing the Diagram & Freeing the Body– ALLOW!

Isolde Nagel

In 2004, when confronted for the first time with José Salinas's topological images of bodies and KNOBSDesign, a new universe opened itself up to me. Design using digital media had left the plane of the pure application of new production techniques and was on the point of generating new spaces of imagination. Upon closer examination, I was fascinated in particular by the apparent freedom from scale which made possible a view of the whole in place of a fragmentary mode of perception; freedom from scale in the sense of a constantly shifting field within which the difference between point and line is suspended. The variables are not accidental, but are instead designed and programmed by Salinas. They refer explicitly to the human body which experiences a continuous adaptation and orientation within a system of external influences. On the basis of the inscribed information model, this topological body is constantly redefined in the computer, and hence experiences a perpetually changing identity. Dynamic interactions between processes of variation, transformation, and mutation compel the beholder to undergo a constant shift of perspective, opening up a diverse field of associations.

A key aspect of José Salinas's artistic/architectonic work is an investigation of the intimate affinity between the body and urban space. In 2008, as a contribution to that year's theme *An intimac(it)y*, Salinas created the temporary installation *Disembodiment* in the A trans Pavilion in Berlin. The curatorial concept of A trans Pavilion envisions the exhibition space as a hybrid: it is a display window, an art space, and an exhibition location, as well as a think tank for investigating cultural paradigms, contemporary lifestyles, and new experimental tendencies in urban practices and identities. Participating associates are invited to conceive and plan projects that go beyond their own disciplines. *An intimac(it)y*, formed of the words Intimacy and City, investigated the significance of the intimate body and its social environment. The body and its extension constitutes the frame of reference for its existence, its own experience, and its interaction with the collective.

In A trans Pavilion, Salinas operates with facts, with the architectonic situation of the pavilion, and with older notions of Euclidean bodies. In the installation, these fuse into a whole, blurring the boundaries between architecture, design, and art. As visitors, we are called upon to enter a spatial experiment of transition—in a search for connections between body, building, and city within and outside of our own skins (envelopes).

With the term *Disembodiment*, Salinas refers in general to a process that divests our bodies of all material existence and changes and transforms their physical states. This transformation allows the separation and the boundary between body and thought to become more clearly perceptible. It is expressed in the becoming strange of one's own body, of bodily perception, and of human behavior. It is interesting for us to attempt to discover whether this boundary is actually perceptible and where it disintegrates again. What if this division between body and thought is merely a construct of consciousness?

Salinas assumes that various urban worlds and living spaces generate the most diverse processes of disembodiment. The environment consists of uncharted forces and synergies which work together through their plenitude and complexity. The body's epidermis, too, acts like an environment, a topological configuration that bestows space and energy. It, too, is dependent upon the complexity of the environment. The human individual is compelled to produce images of itself and of the world. Consciousness processes signals registered by the sensory organs, linking new experiences with the already familiar. Every act of communication is bound up with exchange of energies whose

visualization is nonetheless always linked to notions of containment and form.

In the specific urban situation of the A trans Pavilion, whose interior opens onto its urban surroundings via its display window, it is possible to experience the transformation of the body in a double sense. With his point of departure in this glass-and-concrete cube, Salinas simulates an interior habitat on the scale of 1:1. Visitors "experience" this space, themselves undergoing a process of disembodiment. The plain and symmetrical arrangement of large-format panels and cubes takes up the pavilion's pre-existing spatial structure. Salinas fabricates an environment that channels our awareness initially toward forms and surfaces while at the same time opening up new perspectives. On the elevated level of the glass fiber pedestals, visitors can balance in space, thereby perceiving the physical connection between the surrounding architecture, their bodies, and their own sense of interiority. Deep black Ilfochromes, onto which bodies have been marked out, form a surrounding projection surface. Upon sustained viewing, the delicate greens and whites, the minimally varying contours, evoke not only images of antique doctrines of proportion, but also unfurl an intimate life of their own. Two "formless" entities—one is tempted to identify them as masculine and feminine bodies—refer to topographical configurations.

We can anticipate that soon, science and the computer will be capable of inaugurating entirely new conceptions. Exchanges of energy will no longer be bound to figure and form. To be capable of linking up, without resistance to the transformation of our environment and of our own bodies, would be something marvelous—and would, in fact, transgress boundaries.

Acknowledgements

This book is dedicated to New York City and Madrid; the two cities that allowed me to develop my thoughts and offered me the opportunity to grow personally and intellectually.

I owe many thanks for the realization of this book. It has been a tremendous experience doing this book, and it would not have reached this level of completion without the continuous support of key associates and friends over the years.

Thanks go to the publisher, Jochen Visscher, for his immediate and sustained support of this project.

Isolde Nagel, through continued and indefatigable support of my work and positioning towards architecture over the years, acted as an encouraging presence for tackling the key arguments presented in this book.

I would like to acknowledge the significance of the generous contribution of Anh-Linh Ngo, whose vision established a strong contextualization of my work, and established keynote connections to KNOBSDesign architectural thinking and practice.

I thank Alice Lautenschlager, Swiss print master, who has supported my artwork over the years. Her commitment to excellence, personal engagement producing my artworks, and over forty years of experience working with cibachromes, has been a vital aspect in the development of my art.

I thank my parents Manuela Agudo López and Bernardo Salinas Ramírez whose unconditional support gave me confidence through the years of struggle, and María Antonia Salinas Agudo (Toñi), my sister, a constant reflection in my work.

Finally, I thank Kerstin Grasser for her support and understanding. Her sharp and concise comments are always important to mantain the design process consistency.

KNOBSDesign

KNOBSDesign was founded by José Salinas in New York and also has an office in Madrid. KNOBS is the acronym for Knowledge Based System. Furthermore, KNOBS are the controlling parameters whose intensity defines the dynamical state of the structure-generating process. When KNOBSDesign was conceived, the first thing we decided was to position ourselves in the broad field of architecture as multidisciplinary and collaborative; particularly, within the undefined and intertwining territory between art and architecture. This positioning allowed us to continuously bring our findings on art installations into the architectural design processes, and vice versa; developing rather unique techniques and visions about space and integration of our body within the urban context. Therefore, over the past ten years, we have engaged in experimentation with different media, developing new design methodologies and strategies that led us to adaptable organizational systems that could be implemented at different scales simultaneously. As technology rapidly evolved over the course of our practice, we sought to embrace its creative potential while investigating its cultural and spatial implications through experimental work, which continues to be the most precious aspect of our practice. Indeed, we channeled most of our energies into conducting research for our various building and digital projects—

from the use of new technologies and responsive materials, to issues of urban complexity, building organization, and culture. All of these concurrent pursuits present our drive to tread unknown territories and explore new possibilities for architecture with the aim of expanding the boundaries of traditional architectural practice from buildings and urban design, to gallery installations and augmented interactive environments. All projects are exploring inner living spaces, shaped by external machinist systems of information that transform and generate new topological configurations, and are equally concerned with new types of building systems. KNOBSDesign has completed construction of different projects in New York, and is currently working on different projects in Spain. The work of KNOBSDesign has been exhibited internationally in numerous galleries, including: Weissenhof Architecture Gallery, Stuttgart; A trans Pavilion, Berlin; AedesEast/Extension Pavilion, Berlin; The Architectural Association Gallery, London; Schafler Gallery, Pratt Institute, New York; Taubman College Gallery, University of Michigan; AIA Center for Architecture, New York; Batofar Multimedia Event, Paris; Wi-Fi Royal Gardens, Copenhagen. KNOBSonians: José Salinas, MArch. Principal. Kerstin Grasser, Dipl.-Ing. (FH) Architect+team

Contact: inf@knobsdesign.com

Index & Credits

José Salinas, MArch | AA [DRL, 00]

Selected Projects:
Toroidal Landscapes. Madrid, Spain 2009
Disembodiment, funded. Berlin, Germany 2008
Onishi Gallery / Gallery Memoria, New York 2006/7
Architecture Within. Berlin, Germany 2005
Asymmetrical Body: Spirit Away. New York 2005
Genomic Herm_A(phrodite). New York 2004
Shrinking Cities, competition. Detroit 2004
h1415_6, commissioned. New York 2004
CSV/AAI Centre. New York 2004
Museum in TL-SYNC, competition. South Korea 2003
WTC Memorial, competition. New York 2003
Hermeneutic Topologies. New York 2003
Haptic Maps, commissioned. New York 2003
Ephemeral Structures, competition. Athens 2002
Tono Sci-Research City, competition. Japan 2002

Academic Appointments:
Universidad Europea de Madrid. Escuela Superior de Arte y Arquitectura. Since 2007
Cornell University. College of Architecture, Art & Planning. Visiting Critic. Spring 2007
The Architectural Association. London 2006
Pratt Institute. School of Architecture. New York. Visiting Instructor. Fall 2004
MIT, Massachusetts Institute of Technology. Lecturer in Architecture. Spring 2004
Princeton University. School of Architecture. Digital Media Assistant. 2002-2003

Lectures:
Stuttgart State University of Art&Design. 2008
Universidad Europea de Madrid. Spain 2008
Berlin University of the Arts (UdK). 2008
The Architectural Association. London 2006
Pontificia Univ. Católica. Chile 2006
Frankfurt Academy of Fine Arts. 2005
Instituto Cervantes. Berlin 2005
GSD Harvard. Cambridge 2003

Awards/Grants/Sponsorships:
Ministry of Culture. Madrid, Spain
Spanish Embassy in Berlin. Germany
Seeger & Dürr Stiftung. Stutensee, Germany
Foto-Lautenschlager. St. Gallen, Switzerland
Seeger-Schaltechnik GmbH. Stutensee
ILFOCHROME. Switzerland
Instituto Cervantes Berlin
ILFORD Imaging Switzerland GmbH
Director's Grant, Council for the Arts at MIT

Solo Exhibitions:
Disembodiment. Weissenhof Architecture Gallery. Stuttgart 2008
Disembodiment. A trans Pavilion. Berlin 2008
Architecture Within. AedesEast Gallery. Berlin 2005
Meta-Shiftments. Friedberg Gallery. Berlin 2004

Group Exhibitions:
International Art Fair for Modern and Contemporary Art [FIART]. Valencia, Spain 2008
DRL_TEN. AA Gallery. London, UK 2008
The Thames Gateway Assembly at the AA. AA Gallery. London, UK 2006
E-xtensioni. Naples, Italy 2005
Crossing Disciplines/Drawing. Schafler Gallery. Pratt Institute. Brooklyn, New York 2005
Humanos Artificiales. Galería Artificial. Madrid 2004
The Peekskill Project. Hudson Valley Center for Contemporary Art. Peekskill, New York 2004
3060900506. Taubman College Gallery. University of Michigan 2004
mace2/artists from the flat file. The:Artist:Network. New York 2004
eMeRGeNT04/05. AIANY Center for Architecture. New York 2004
Downtown Digitalia NYC. Paris 2003
New//Orb Remote Wifi. Royal Gardens, Copenhagen 2003
A World New Media Blender Event & Exhibition. Arts International. New York 2003
You Are Here. Diesel Denim Gallery. New York 2003
Lebensraum/Homeland Insecurity. The:Artist: Network. New York 2003

Publications:
Disembodiment. Architektur:Positionen. jovis Verlag. Berlin 2009

Embedded Within in 306090 10. Princeton Architectural Press (PAPress). New York 2006
Crossing Disciplines/Drawing, Artist's Statements Sketchbook. Schafler Gallery. New York 2005
Afterward: Scaleless Urbanism, Pamphlet Architecture No. 26. PAPress. New York 2004
Shiftments, 306090 05. PAPress. New York 2003

Reviews:
Onishi Gallery/Gallery Memoria, in *1000XArchitecture of the Americas*. Verlagshaus Braun. Berlin 2008
Multi-Linear Fields, in *DRL TEN: A Design Research Compendium*. AA Publications. London 2008
Seminal Space: Getting Under the Digital Skin, A. Imperiale, in *Re: Skin*. MIT Press. Boston 2007
Onishi Gallery/Gallery Memoria, in issue 05, *The Architect's Newspaper*. New York 2006
Multi-Linear Fields, in *Corporate Fields: New Office Environments by the AA DRL*. AA Publications. London 2005
A conversation with José Salinas, in *306090 05*. PAPress. New York 2003

Architecture selected projects credits:
Toroidal Landscapes. Madrid 2009, pp. 119-125
Architect: José Salinas
Images: KNOBSDesign
Disembodiment, solo installation.
A trans Pavilion. Berlin 2008, pp. 76-82, 137
Architect: José Salinas Curator: Isolde Nagel
Onishi Gallery / Gallery Memoria. 521W 26th St., Chelsea, New York 2007, pp. 68-74
Client: Yagiken, Co. Ltd., Memoria, Inc.
Architect: José Salinas

Museum in TL-SYNC - competition.
South Korea 2003, pp. 13, 48-59
Architects: José Salinas, Markus Randler
Images: KNOBSDesign
Intelligent Surface: Multimedia Platform for 2004 Olympic Games - competition. 2002, pp. 41-47
Architects: José Salinas, Noboru Ota
Images: KNOBSDesign
Glowing Topologies. Tono Frontier Science Research City - competition. Japan 2002, pp. 30-35
Architects: José Salinas, Markus Randler
Images: KNOBSDesign
Multi-Linear Fields. London 2000, pp. 19-29
Architects: José Salinas, Juan I. Aranguren

Photo credits:

Disembodiment. A trans Pavilion. Berlin
Photographers: Hiepler, Brunier, pp. 76-82
Photographer: Christiane Kretschmer, p.137
Onishi Gallery/Gallery Memoria. New York
Photographer: Seong Kwon, pp. 68-74

Artworks (selected):

Original works by José Salinas. Cibachromes.
Seeking Portrait. 2003. 43.2 x 58.5cm, pp.102-103
Hermeneutic Topologies. 2004. Polyptych. 43.2 x 58.5cm, pp. 108-111
Asymmetrical Body: Spirit Away. 2005. Diptych. 250 x 100cm, p. 90
Couple. 2008. Diptych. 250 x 100cm, p. 91
Female. 2008. Polyptych. 250 x 100cm, pp.128-129
Female Heads. 2008. 250 x 100cm, pp. 130-131
Male Heads. 2008. 250 x 100cm, pp. 132-134
Body_024_080. 2009. 250 x 100cm, pp. 92-93

MyOthers. 2009. 43.2 x 58.5cm, pp. 104-107
Listening Bodies Series. 2009, pp. 112-117
Listening Bodies_1.000. 125 x 150cm
Listening Bodies_0.900. 125 x 150cm
Listening Bodies_0.450. 125 x 150cm
Listening Bodies_0.300. 125 x 150cm
Listening Bodies_0.200. 125 x 150cm
Listening Bodies_0.150. 125 x 150cm
Sinchronic Bodies Series. 2009, pp. 94-101
Sinchronic Bodies_1.000. 150 x 100cm
Sinchronic Bodies_0.900. 150 x 100cm
Sinchronic Bodies_0.500. 150 x 100cm
Sinchronic Bodies_0.450. 150 x 100cm
Sinchronic Bodies_0.400. 150 x 100cm
Sinchronic Bodies_0.300. 150 x 100cm
Sinchronic Bodies_0.250. 150 x 100cm
Sinchronic Bodies_0.200. 150 x 100cm

KNOBSDesign. New York_Madrid